POLYWORKER

POLYWORKER

DITCH THE CORPORATE LADDER AND REINVENT
YOUR CAREER ON YOUR TERMS

Brie Abramowicz

POLYWORKER: DITCH THE CORPORATE LADDER AND REINVENT YOUR CAREER ON YOUR TERMS

ISBN: 979-8-9938861-0-7

Published by Human Factors Press

Printed in the United States of America

Find out more at www.buildwithbrie.com

Mille grazie to my OG professional polycule,

Linda, MJ, Nicole, Paige, Tarryn, John, Corinne, Shaina, Patrick, Maureen, Bradley, Anneliese, and of course, "my shmoops." This book, and my portfolio career, would've fallen apart somewhere around "draft three" if not for your encouragement and support.

TABLE OF CONTENTS

INTRODUCTION BY JAVAREE WALKER

The first time I stumbled across Brie's words, I wasn't necessarily looking for clarity. I was scrolling LinkedIn in a moment in my career where I felt like I was barely keeping my head above water—trying to keep up with the demands of my job, processing the news of more rounds of layoffs in the tech world, and navigating the swirl of emotions and logistics that came with preparing for the birth of my second child. I remember stopping to read one of her posts because it sounded like she was saying the thing out loud that so many of us were holding inside (or at least I was). She had written about losing her job, suddenly feeling disconnected from her community, and about the way our identity can unravel when the job we've tied our worth to disappears.

I had been laid off in the past and understood this particular form of grief. But this moment in modern work felt different. I'd watched many of my friends reel from sudden losses, trying to rebuild their sense of belonging. At the same time, what had felt stable in my own career suddenly didn't feel so certain as I prepared for my paternity leave. The ground beneath me felt as if it was shifting, and the mix of emotions I carried was heavy. There was frustration, and a restless sense of "what now." I hadn't verbalized it to anyone else yet, but I felt like there was more there to be explored.

Reading that post obviously didn't fix anything, but it sparked something open in me, and it led me to take action and start working with Brie. It was like she had snuck into my inner sanctum and said, "Hey, I see you. And I can help."

We explored how I felt like I was learning more from family life than from anywhere else. The small lessons that came from watching a little one explore the world, pausing to notice things, to question them, and experience new forms of joy, were shaping me as much as any professional milestone ever had. And it left me with so much I wanted to share about being a parent. I felt a pull to speak more broadly, to educate, and to inspire others with what I was discovering about work, parenting, and identity. But because of my own all-or-nothing thinking trap, I didn't know how to make it work. I couldn't see how to integrate that desire to share my experience as a father with the desire to relentlessly "achieve" at work. My internal dialogue was relentless.

How do I do this? Do I even *want* to do this? What would it look like to honor what I felt called to say and still meet the demands of my day job when I returned to work? I didn't have answers, but I knew value alignment mattered deeply to me. And when I thought about my core values, curiosity had always risen to the top. Reading Brie's words and working with her during that time reminded me that exploration itself has value.

As I continued to follow her digital content over the next eighteen months, I began to notice something beyond the words themselves: a community was taking shape in response to them. Through this space she had created, I connected with people asking the same questions that I was: Was there another way to live and work that didn't require sacrificing family or other parts of our identity? Could we have more work-life integration?

Through those conversations, I began to feel less alone. New relationships grew from this community's shared struggle, but also from its shared vision for what work could become.

It's one thing to read a story and nod in recognition. It's another to meet others who carry that same story in their own way. Being part of that community showed me how many of us are quietly navigating similar transitions, even if the details look different. In Brie's community, I met seasoned entrepreneurs and executives that were also just starting out in their career reinvention journey. We had something in common: we were unraveling old narratives that we had been conditioned to accept, letting go of the idea that work must consume us, and trying to rebuild something more humane in its place.

When I picked up *Polyworker*, it felt like an extension of these community conversations. Brie's writing takes you to an even more intimate and reflective place inside her first year of building a portfolio career, along with all the uncertainty, excitement, unease, and fear that came with it. Reading it feels like sitting down with a friend who was willing to tell the truth about what it takes to start over.

This book offered me language—not just vocabulary—a way to describe the quiet disorientation I'd been carrying.

As I read it, I found myself reminded of something Thoreau wrote: "The mass of men lead lives of quiet desperation." That line has always haunted me, but reading *Polyworker* reminded me that naming the desperation is perhaps the first step toward escaping it.

Consider reading *Polyworker* the way I read it, not as an instructional manual, but as a conversation with a friend. Imagine sitting across from Brie at a coffee shop with a warm mug in your hands and feeling nervous to admit what's really been on your mind about your work. Imagine her looking back at you and telling a story that makes your shoulders drop and your breath come a little easier. That's what her writing and coaching have done for me, and that's what I hope it does for you too.

Polyworker isn't about achievement per se. It's about our humanity. And what it feels like to acknowledge the need for a change, to make one, and still keep going even when it gets hard.

So as you turn the pages, I hope you give yourself the same gift I did, which is to slow down, to get curious about your experience, and to let yourself be seen in someone else's story. You don't have to have it all figured out. You don't need a master plan. You only need a little bit of space to breathe and the courage to ask yourself, "What now?"

So yeah, grab that cup, and let Brie's words meet you where you are!

UNRAVELING

HOW TO READ THIS BOOK

So you picked up this book, which means you're probably having one of those, "WHAT THE HELL AM I DOING WITH MY LIFE?" moments that makes you want to set your laptop on fire and run away to live in a yurt somewhere remote with no WiFi.

Let me take a wild guess here: you did everything "right." Got the fancy degree, climbed that damn corporate ladder, and collected a series of job titles that you thought would sound impressive at your high school reunion.

Welcome to the club. The membership will cost you your sanity, but we've got pretty good snacks.

I wrote this book *for you*.

Two things you should know before you dive in:

First, you deserve honesty about what the portfolio career model of work asks of its participants. Not some guru bullshit where you are peddled frameworks for navigating career transitions that look as easy as making a smoothie. We need more truth and fewer people trying to sell us magic beans, okay?

Second, there's plenty of material out there about the business mechanics of building a portfolio career. But I did my best to make this book a two-for-one deal that also addresses the emotional shitstorm of inner work that happens in parallel to building one.

Over the next however-many pages, I'm going to overshare about my own beautiful disaster of building a portfolio career in real time so you can see what it's really like in the first few years. I want you to know that it's totally okay to be frustrated, furious, and hopeful all at the same time. That this cocktail of emotions is just the price of admission for doing creative, meaningful work in a world that wasn't exactly designed for unconventional careers—let alone at this particularly weird moment in human history.

So . . . with that in mind . . .

Here's what this book is NOT going to do:

- Give you some bullshit five-step plan for building a six-figure business from your couch.

- Promise you "passive income" or teach you how to "hustle your way to freedom" (ugh, even typing that made me throw up a little). *or*

- Tell you to quit your job tomorrow and "follow your bliss" into financial ruin*.

But here's what it IS going to do:

- Give you the words for those feelings you've been carrying around but couldn't quite name.

- Tell you stories that'll hopefully make you laugh, think, and feel seen in whatever weird career transition you're swimming through right now.

- Offer you the companionship of someone who's been exactly where you are—stuck in that uncomfortable space between who everyone told you to be and who you're brave enough to finally become, *and*

- Eventually (in Act III and IV), prompt reflection and action pertaining to a few broad themes that I've noticed are common challenges for people like us. (We're an *us* now, by the way *wink*)

My story isn't thrown in here because it's particularly unique—it's in here because it contains themes that will sound familiar to my fellow Millennials (up top, guys!). I'm sharing them to show you how I developed the theories and perspectives that inform my coaching practice and business philosophy. If you've worked in different industries or you're from a different generation, you've probably experienced different flavors of the same challenges.

I should also note that part of my story involves getting my business practice up and running. I've done a bit of creative anonymizing when I reference the experiences of my clients and professional friends (and enemies) throughout the book—I do this out of respect as confidentiality boundaries are important for me to maintain.

We're all trying to build lives that actually work for the world we live in now—a world that looks nothing like the one our parents prepared us for. The old career playbook doesn't apply anymore, and we're in the middle of writing a new one. So we're basically out here in these career streets, improvising, making it up as we go, and imagining what comes next.

And that, my friend, is going to take some serious fucking courage.

With love and solidarity,
Brie

We're all trying to build lives that work for the world we live in now—a world that looks nothing like the one our parents prepared us for.

CHAPTER ONE

MY SO-CALLED MILLENNIAL MIDLIFE CRISIS

December 2023

- ✓ Current employment status: 0 jobs
- ✓ Christmas spirit level: Grinch-adjacent
- ✓ Wine consumed: Festive "Wisconsin family gathering" amounts (somber yet celebratory!)
- ✓ Times I've practiced saying "I'm exploring new opportunities" in the mirror: 23

So. Here I am. Sitting in my car in the company parking lot like some sort of corporate refugee, which is exactly as pathetic as it sounds.

There's a calendar invite that ominously appeared on my phone thirty minutes ago like a digital death sentence. Fifteen minutes. Private. Starts in ninety seconds.

You know what's funny? I'd actually considered *not* going into the office today. Just driving away in my car forever because, well, I hate this place. But then I remembered I have a mortgage and student loans to pay, so... again, here I am.

The attendee list for said meeting is concerning.

There's Trish from HR who I find annoying. Trish is the kind of adult who I am convinced has a *Live, Laugh, Love* poster on display in every room of her home.

The other person on the invite is my boss's boss, which is never–*and I mean never*–a good sign.

I rush inside. Fully flushed. And stress pitted out.

The mood in the conference room where the three of us are apparently gathering is already somber as I walk in.

FUCKKKKKKK.

"This isn't personal," Trish says, sliding a sizable pile of papers to sign across the table. "Your position has been eliminated. We're restructuring."

This is the part where I should cry, isn't it? Have some sort of dignified emotional response? Maybe throw something at Trish out of spite?

I can see myself already–updating LinkedIn with that tragic "Open to opportunities!" banner that might as well scream "WILL TRADE DIGNITY FOR HEALTHCARE."

But instead of grief, I feel . . . relief.

Like, actual oxygen-returning-to-my-lungs relief. I am either unfazed or having a psychological breakdown so complete, it's disguised as mental clarity.

Either way, I don't have to pretend that "creating cross-functional synergies" or "optimizing for stakeholder engagement" matters to me anymore.

I stand up in excitement and knock over Trish's water bottle. Its contents begin to empty on her laptop. Classic. Go me! Accidentally sticking it to the man! I pause before walking through the office doorway, affording one last glance at the office I'd sold my soul to for the past 36 months. Through the comically oversized fishbowl windows, I watch them—the chosen ones—hunched over their screens like obedient lab rats. No one looks up from their computers to say goodbye.

Of course not.

My phone buzzes. Text from my husband: "How did it go?"

Saying, "I've been made redundant," feels about as truthful as calling explosive diarrhea "tummy troubles."

I freeze at the screen, thumb hovering, brain buffering. My body's already halfway out the door, but my mind is still here, spiraling through a mental carousel of drafted, deleted, re-drafted replies. Finally, like the neurotic human I am, I land on, "I'm freeee?"—complete with an over-the-top GIF for dramatic effect.

It's two weeks until Christmas. Clearly what Santa's workshop was missing this year was yet another unemployed, workaholic, elder millennial with $80 grand in outstanding student loans.

Sign me up, Santa. Mama needs work!

———

I'd been living a lie. Cosplaying as a functioning adult in Corporate America for the last 7 years of my career . . . give or take a handful of performance reviews.

And it wasn't even the sexy double-life kind of lie where you have a secret pair of children in Vermont and a burner phone in your gym bag. No, this was the slow, insidious type—the kind where you whisper the same story to yourself so often that it becomes gospel.

Until one day, you blink.

And then you find yourself in a conference room full of conformists just like you, nodding along with the CEO like a sea of bobbleheads, while thinking, *"Surely, this isn't my life. This is a stock photo of my life. And worse—I think someone else picked the filter!"*

The success narrative I was sold when I was 18 went a little something like: Play the game. Play the *corporate* game. Smile in meetings. Keep your eyebrows symmetrical! And the gods of Corporate Olympus will reward your loyalty with promotions, a raise, and maybe—just maybe—a complimentary salad four times a year at Company All Hands events.

I chugged the Kool-Aid and asked for seconds. I marinated in that myth. I practically licked the ladle. Hook, line, and sucker!

During those years of corporate discontent, I kept thinking that I was the problem.

That if I just found the *right* company, with the *right* boss, in the *right* role, with a communal fridge that actually stocked the right LaCroix, everything would click. (Tangerine, obvi. Fuck lime, it goes flat too fast!) So I bounced around like some kind of professional Goldilocks, repeatedly convincing myself that the next job would be different. But all I was really doing was collecting blazers I hated for jobs that gave me Sunday Scaries so intense that they started on Friday afternoons.

Some people (maybe you, dear reader) will call this a midlife crisis. You need to know that I hate that term with the fire of a thousand suns. It's so dismissive. I would like to politely punch people who use it in the metaphorical kneecaps. Seriously, why is questioning the fundamental assumptions of your adult life some kind of psychological failing?

As if it's shameful to freak out when you notice that twenty years of your professional career turned out completely different than advertised. Why is pattern recognition a character flaw, exactly? Tell me, please, I'm curious.

Because here's what I think is happening to us American knowledge workers with fancy email signatures and a mild caffeine dependency. We were convinced we were going to change the world. None of our teachers warned us that we'd start measuring our worth by how fast we could answer emails while peeing. That we'd become the kinds of people who whisper to their kid at bedtime, *"Sorry, dear I have to stop reading to you now. Brad from accounting is asking Mommy to explain our Q3 churn."*

Since then, we've lived through a laundry list of "once-in-a-lifetime" events . . . *multiple* times: The Dot-Com Bubble, 9/11, the 2008 financial meltdown, the COVID pandemic, climate doom, the slow death of democracy, collapsing public institutions, and the enshitification of too many social media platforms to count. We've come to realize that our fantasies of success take place in a world that no longer exists, if it ever did.

So why *did* I stay in that shitty job?

I believe I stayed because it was comfortable-*ish*. It looked impressive on LinkedIn. It paid me disgustingly well. And (I hate admitting this part) I stayed because I was *good* at it. Good at playing the role of the polished, dependable, high-achieving corporate employee.

And I thought if I left, if I walked away from the title, the team, and the Tuesday morning meetings that broke my spirit, it meant I had somehow *failed* in my career.

But at a certain point, your intuition gets so loud that it overpowers the corporate elevator muzak that's been playing in your head.

So when it came time to update my resume for this unexpected job hunt, it felt like writing an obituary for a stranger.

I decided I wanted out of *waves at all of* this.

I needed to have a proper think about my ridiculous, painful, oddly hilarious career history to piece together how exactly I had arrived *here*.

But at a certain point, your intuition gets so loud that it overpowers the corporate elevator muzak that's been playing in your head.

I graduated college in 2006, choosing to delay "real life" by taking part in a short-term Peace Corps-style program in rural Mexico. I volunteered for a small nonprofit in a town in the beautiful outskirts of Oaxaca, which had been unfortunately hollowed out by free trade, corruption, and the drug war. Eighty percent of the men from Santa Cruz Papalutla–fathers, brothers, sons–had left behind their families and loved ones in their pursuit of a better life in the US.

I am still to this day deeply appreciative of this experience. I think it planted the early seed of systems-thinking in my brain, forcing me to open my eyes and see the underbelly of globalization and the real people and places behind these abstract economic forces. Until that particular experience, I never realized how much the negative effects of capitalism could shape someone's day-to-day life.

The next year, I moved on to gainful employment in a glass-and-concrete tower in North Carolina–working as a financial analyst for a big bank–immersed in fluorescent lights and six-figure gripes. When I joined that graduate analyst program, I struggled to make sense of the entitlement I witnessed on a daily basis. Only a few months prior, I had no access to running water. And now I was surrounded by junior executives complaining about the drink limits at the company happy hours and their lackluster bonuses.

Then things got even more weird.

I was appointed to an analyst's post on the mergers-and-acquisitions team for what many within the firm were calling "the deal of the century:" the acquisition of

Countrywide Financial. For those who are unfamiliar, Countrywide sat at the heart of the 2008 housing crash and was one of the biggest contributors to the subprime mortgage meltdown that nearly tanked the global economy. Alongside a cohort of other young recruits, I suddenly found myself in the conference rooms where the fallout was supposedly being "managed"—in name, perhaps, but certainly not in justice.

Over the next two years, I served on a vast team charged with dismantling what remained of the bank and absorbing it into its new parent company's operations. The work was both procedural and monumental.

Most days, it felt surreal.

Like when our team had to spend 6 months understanding the inner workings of the infamous "Friends of Angelo" program—a secret VIP program where D.C. politicians and Hollywood heroes scored sweetheart mortgage rates in exchange for looking the other way while the company vacuumed cash from working-class families. Or that one morning in 2011 when my team processed Warren Buffett's $5 billion lifeline to save the banking industry from collapse, treating it with the calm of processing a routine utility bill payment. And then there was the kerfuffle of what to do with the CEO's pet tiger (Angelo Mozilo who I mentioned earlier), which was perched in the company's lobby like some sort of spirit animal. Turns out tigers don't liquidate well.

And after all of that? The banks carried on with business as usual, just with a few new compliance checklists brought to them by Sarbanes-Oxley.

Meanwhile, the middle class in America lost their homes. And their pensions.

I didn't have words for it then, but I do now: I had just enjoyed a front-row seat to one of the greatest wealth transfers (and moral bankruptcies) of my lifetime. It wasn't just a failure of financial markets; it was a breach of a moral and social contract.

It was a formative experience to say the least.

All this systemic rot wrapped in a pretty 401(k) seemed so divorced from the world I grew up in, where I watched my parents run honest small businesses in carpet cleaning and construction. I wasn't used to unfettered capitalism, I was used to community-based commerce, where value was tangible and mutually beneficial, and where bad actors suffered consequences.

I spent the rest of my 20s after that experience dicking around professionally, working in dry finance roles and partying a lot. Some of that was the natural indulgence of youth. But it was also because I didn't know how to metabolize what I'd witnessed right out of college. And so, almost unconsciously, I distanced myself from a deeply American conviction—that a job is not only what we do, but who we are.

Then I discovered Michael Pollan and the good food movement and quickly became enamored of this new philosophy of business: the triple bottom line of profit, people, and planet. Talks of "slow food!" And from these hifalutin ideas a new corporate governance structure was birthed: the B Corporation. There were finally businesses that claimed to care about more than profit and scale. Wow!

So I enrolled in business school, hungry to participate in building a better future. I got my start in the food industry at Target and then moved into a coveted gig at a "sustainable" seafood company with a vision to distribute its products nationally. On paper, that gig represented everything I wanted: a role in a values-led, mission-driven, company that was environmentally conscious.

And yet, one question kept nagging at me while I worked there: *Why exactly did we need to grow the company so damn aggressively?*

The other employees debated this too, but unfortunately our investors were hungry for their 5–10x returns. So growth and scale became our mandate, even though that's not terribly B Corp-like. I pretty quickly realized that the dream I was sold by those greenwashed venture capitalists of a more "patient form of capital" was complete bollocks. The venture capital business was taking the food industry out to lunch.

By the time I was 35, I was constantly wondering: *Is this really it?*

I simply couldn't tether my career to yet another company that dressed up extraction in prettier fonts.

———

It was at this point that I decided to pivot to tech. Not out of hope, but out of a sense of realism. I told myself that, at the very least, the technology was interesting, and the pay would be decent. I didn't need the mission anymore, and I really couldn't stand the cognitive dissonance of the better food movement. Plus I wanted the same paychecks those rich tech bros seemed to be making, so I could buy myself that compound in the woods some day!

But the pay faucet ran dry.

Interest rates spiked.

Capital investments cooled.

And in 2023 I was laid off—unexpectedly.

And a creeping panic consumed my body before my mind could catch up.

It was oh-so-familiar, the same panic of 2008, of 2017, and of 2020.

I was overwhelmed by a profound sense of grief.

It was deep. Cellular.

And this time around, I couldn't push the feelings away. They screamed from my conscious brain demanding to be known while I mindlessly clicked apply on over hundreds of full-time job applications, hoping an employer would cho-cho-chooooose me.

This also happened to be the season where AI hype began flooding social platform feeds.

I started witnessing a whole cohort of fellow tech employees that I had begun casually coaching push past their compounded trauma (of COVID, the 2023/24 layoffs, DEI backlash, and now being voluntold to adopt AI quickly).

"Increase your output please."

"Trim those costs."

"And make sure to justify that you can't do the job first with AI before we approve your FTE request!!"

(All just to keep your current job btw.)

And outside the virtual walls of these successful companies making public declarations about AI? Everyone in tech seemed to be breaking a bit. We screamed at each other on social platforms in a state of self-righteousness about em-dashes. (WTF? Of all the things to get on a soap box about, that's what we picked?!)

And questions about our deepest existential concerns—the loss of meaning and our impending professional obsolescence—began saturating the cultural dialogue.

I, like you, became consumed by the ambient anxiety of this daily paradox we were living through; I simultaneously wanted to be a productive member of society and to feel whole again. And, for once in my god damned adult life, for the work systems I participated in to feel humane.

I wasn't actually anti-AI. I was just fucking tired.

And I wanted a new operating system free of the posturing bullshit.

What I didn't know was that I was headed into a whole new world of chaos.

CHAPTER TWO

MAD MEN LIVING IN A TIKTOK WORLD

February 2024

I'm two months into *fun*employment.

Most days start by mindlessly doomscrolling to avoid applying to jobs.

And then I see it. A TikTok. It's a snippet of an interview with the CEO of that AI darling startup with a vague, derivative name. SynerTechify or something like that.

He's young. He's white. Smugger than a philosophy major who just discovered Nietzsche. And he is sitting in a San Francisco high-rise, talking directly into the camera, nervously fondling his fidget spinner like it's a rosary.

The spinner catches the light—round and round and round it goes—until suddenly I'm syncing up with his nervous system, two broken metronomes keeping the same pathetic beat.

"At SynerTechify," the CEO says, shifting awkwardly back and forth in his chair, "we believe AI is going to change the world."

Oh, fuck off. This sociopathic Muppet probably laid off ten thousand people last week, and now he's preaching tech gospel like he's the Pope of Productivity. What's next–baptizing me with Soylent? A wafer shaped like a QR code?

I glance around my home office, half-expecting hidden cameras. Is this a bit? Some sort of social experiment?

He keeps going, mouth full of buzzwords, fidget spinner now a glowing halo. And I realize: I am watching a man audition for sainthood in the Church of Sam Altman.

Blessed be the algorithm.

AI is our salvation.

Bow your heads and invest in our Series B.

I slam my laptop shut. Then I sit there and stare at the wall. In what world does this freshly minted man-boy's tropes make any sense?

And in the silence–this slow-simmering stew of rage–it finally hit me.

I'm not just done with this silly techbro.

I'm done with the entire circus that built his tent.

The whole rotten deal of late-stage capitalism, where you sacrifice your sleep, your sanity, your personality for some contrived pinnacle of "success" that ends with . . . what? A corner office? Private panic attacks on the company's dime?

No. Thank. You.

I began habitually rewatching the entire series of *Mad Men* after being laid off. Like I was an understudy preparing for all of the possible roles I could play in the theater of corporate.

There is a strange comfort in the world of *Mad Men*. Don Draper pacing through the immaculate company corridors, a cigarette at parade rest. Roger Sterling tossing off wit like confetti. Peggy Olson learning to speak in the language of power before the language admits her into the conversation. Corporate life, rendered in mid-century tones, is improbably seductive on screen.

At its core, the show is a meditation on the power of storytelling in service of an idea–the selling of a belief system, the dream of American capitalism itself. As Don explains without saying it: you are not buying a Hershey bar; you are buying the memory of love. You are not buying a Kodak Carousel; you are buying yesterday. You are not buying a hamburger; you are buying time with your family. The transaction is never merely financial; it is sacramental. The pitch is a liturgy. The brand is a creed.

Mad Men isn't simply nostalgia; it's a mirror. It juxtaposes a carefully constructed past with the present and asks us to notice the wallpaper under the wallpaper. The smoke, the sexism, the sanctioned hierarchies– however alluring in their cinematic order–mask deeper rot. And slowly, over seven seasons, we watch an agency sell us a vision of the good life while hollowing out the lives of the people who labor to produce it.

That's why it hits so hard now in my, again, *fun*employment. Because *Mad Men* is a time machine, one that doesn't just move backwards and forwards through the 1960s and 70s. But one that drags us into the present too. It forces us to confront the truth that corporate life and the American Dream has always been a kind of advertising campaign: polished, intoxicating, yet utterly hollow if you look at it too closely.

And for me, somewhere between Don's Lucky Strike Sermon on the Mount and Peggy's cardiganed ascension, I recognized the parallel to my own career. The cult of corporate wasn't just selling me a job. It was selling me a secular faith. Watching the show was comforting, in part, because it revealed this truth. Even the inequities it depicted–misogyny among them–had the appearance of order, of a system whose clarity, however unjust, stood in contrast to the disorder of the present.

I don't for a second want to return to the 1950s or 60s. God no. (Hard pass on girdles and not having my own credit card.) But some part of me–the part that once believed in Corporate America–understood, after re-watching *Mad Men* so many times, that success was never a clean game built on skill and luck. It was always theater. I'd been sold a lie just as surely as Don and Peggy.

And so every belief I had about work, success, and self had to be recontextualized.

For the record, the irony of this isn't lost on me. Women literally fought for my right to work outside the home– burned bras, broke glass ceilings! And here I am, inside my home, in yoga pants, at 11:30 p.m. on a Wednesday, begrudgingly replying to interview requests.

During the first three months of my sabbatical, I started talking to others orbiting the same mid-career crisis. Most were tech workers, but the pattern was undeniable: our optimism had dried up.

Every conversation carried the same refrain. We were miserable at work and convinced we were "behind" where we should be by now. Our personal lives were buckling under the weight of bills, child care, and aging parents. We were all, to some degree, professionally dead inside.

At first, I chalked this up to age—or maybe a kind of pandemic hangover. A low-grade *what's the point of any of this* fever that settles in after two years of botched sourdough starters and confiding in your houseplants. I assumed we'd snap out of it, go back to brunch, and learn to tolerate our corporate jobs again.

But the more I listened to my friends, the more it became clear: this wasn't pandemic burnout.

It was something deeper—a slow, quiet collapse of faith in the promises of Corporate America and the middle-class dream. It was intersectional: racism, sexism, classism, all the isms. Layered with phobias, supremacies, and the gnawing sense that the old success narratives no longer held up.

The corporate ladder wasn't just a structure; it was a symbol of unwavering faith. The altar where we tithed our twenties and thirties in exchange for stability, status, and maybe a retirement condo in Palm Springs.

We were all having that, *"Hey, wait a minute . . ."* moment.

And now the altar stood empty. The priest had been laid off. And the hymns were sung in jargon no one even pretended to understand anymore.

Every conversation felt like sitting together in a pew long after the service had ended. As if we were lingering in restless silence, trading sideways glances, waiting for someone–anyone–to stand up and declare, "It's over."

Because it was. The faith had gone. And once you've lost the faith, you can't un-lose it.

The question is no longer, "*How do we climb the ladder?*"

The question is, "If the religion of corporate is dead, what comes next?"

In that sense, *Mad Men* as a show is punctilious about its era–the typewriters, the ashtrays, the girdles–but it was written with an eye on the present. The anxiety we attribute to the 1960's belongs as easily to 2008, to 2020, and to now. The mood of exhaustion, low self-esteem, the fret about America's place in the world–none of that stayed in black-and-white. It bled into our present.

What changes is not the human condition so much as the interface. Yesterday's Lucky Strike is today's dopamine loop. Yesterday's carousel is today's nostalgia reel. The ad man gave way to the algorithm, which is only a man by other means. The pitch is still the pitch. It just arrives faster, dressed in your preferences.

This is why the show's moral discomfort lingers after the conclusion of its last season. In one season, Joan is asked to barter her dignity for a partnership stake; the deal is repugnant and legible. In our careers, the bargains are ambient. The exchange lives in the terms of service, the after-hours Slacks, the series of "reasonable" compromises you consent to because everyone else does. If mid-century patriarchy was explicit, twenty-first century precarity is exquisitely polite.

And yet—the show offers a counterpoint to despair in the figure of Peggy, not because she wins cleanly but because she compounds success patiently. She does not become Don in a skirt. She becomes herself, season by season, pitch by pitch, in an ecosystem designed to tell her what she cannot be. Watching her, I recognized a different kind of progress than corporate taught me to admire. Not the big reveal but the slow turn. Not the viral moment but the craft that accumulates meaning over time.

There is a temptation, after a layoff, to find a villain or to write a single turning point that reorders the soul. But life is more circular than that.

Don's greatest enemy is not a rival; it is repetition. He returns to the same doors until he learns to stop knocking. We repeat to master or we repeat until it masters us.

This is where my rewatching changed from comfort to inquiry.

What if the way out is not the plot twist but the practice? What if the opposite of corporate as religion is not irreligion but a different liturgy—a life ordered by a body of work instead of a brand, by sovereignty instead of status? What if the antidote to a collapsing faith is not a new idol but a new rhythm?

When people lose traditional religion, they do not stop believing; belief migrates. In the twentieth century, for many Americans, it rooted itself in corporations. The firm offered meaning, ritual, calendar. You knew when to dress up, when to confess, and when to feast. The paycheck was a sacrament. The retirement party, a last rite. In time, the pews thinned.

Institutional decline has its precedents—the late '60s and early '70s saw trust in government crater under the stress of war and scandal; later, the Great Recession stripped the story from finance. Today, layoffs arrive by email, and the machines that brought us together to build something—anything—now measure us and ask us to produce content about our production. The ritual remains. The spirit leaves.

Which is why *Mad Men*'s last grace note matters more than television. "What's the job?" Peggy asks Don. His answer: "Living in the not knowing." It is a terrifying instruction until you choose to hear it as permission.

We are not promised certainty.

But we are offered seasons.

The question is no longer, "How do we climb the ladder?" The question is, "If the religion of corporate is dead, what comes next?"

CHAPTER THREE

THE SIX BETRAYALS OF CORPORATE

March 2024

My home office needed a makeover. You know: new energy, new vigor. Or at least fewer piles of crap threatening to collapse on me during Zoom calls.

I was knee-deep in my archaeological dig when I unearthed a shoebox stuffed with old lanyards, conference paraphernalia, and a couple of cheap "excellence" awards. Proof that, once upon a time, I belonged. Proof that I was useful. Or at least . . . busy.

I held one of the awards up to the light and chuckled. Heavy enough to knock someone out, but worthless now—a monument to late nights and missed birthdays. Years of work distilled into blocks of plastic I was about to throw away.

These weren't souvenirs of success.

They were artifacts of self-betrayal.

Okay, bear with me—I'm about to take a nerdy detour before we return to torching Corporate America.

Do you know John and Julie Gottman? The rockstars of marriage research? They can predict divorce with 90% accuracy just by watching couples argue for fifteen minutes. Fifteen minutes!

In their decades of research on marriage, John and Julie Gottman discovered a set of recurring patterns that proved strikingly predictive. They found that when four particular dynamics appeared together in a relationship—criticism, contempt, defensiveness, and stonewalling—the bond between partners was almost certainly headed toward dissolution. The Gottmans came to call these dynamics *The Four Horsemen of Marriage*, an allusion to the biblical image of impending apocalypse. Their insight was stark but clear: when these forces converge, the end of the relationship is not a matter of possibility but of eventuality.

Which led me to wonder: might the same be true of our relationship with work? Could there be, within the constructs of Corporate America, a set of forces so corrosive that their convergence renders the relationship beyond repair?

I believe there are such forces. Not four, as in the Gottmans' schema, but six—each a harbinger of decline in the faith we once placed in the institutions of work and the promises of the American Dream. If work is a kind of secular faith, then what follows are the six forces that break the covenant.

I call them *The Six Betrayals of Corporate.*

They are:

1. Economic Precarity

2. Invisible Labor

3. Time Theft

4. Perverse Incentives

5. Loss of Purpose

6. Self-Censure

My theory is simple: when all six betrayals converge in your career, you're not just tired.
You're *done*.

Betrayal #1: Economic Precarity

The Myth: Hard work equals stability and economic prosperity.

Did you know that in 1960, a director for an ad agency made about $15,000? That's $150,000 in today's money. The Westchester house Don Draper buys in Season 3 of *Mad Men*? It cost him $19,000—about 1.3 times his annual salary. Today, that same house sells for $800,000.

The present-day creative director in Manhattan might make $200,000 if they're lucky, making the price of that house 4x their pre-tax income. And this financial picture doesn't even factor in what didn't exist as major expenses back then: $2,000/month daycare (In the 1960s, 70% of

American households lived comfortably on one income and didn't need to outsource childcare—more on that soon), a $50,000/yr college tuition per kid, or $500/month health insurance premiums. Today's $200K comes with a 401k you fund yourself and the constant threat of "rightsizing."

So, when you think about it, we didn't just lose buying power. We lost an entire way of life. The promise that hard work leads to prosperity? That died, along with Don Draper's famous three-martini lunch.

Despite all this evidence that tells us the financial odds are against us, we're still telling ourselves that if we just work harder, smarter, longer, everything will work out. And that we still have a safety net.

Even people making six figures are living paycheck-to-paycheck now. I hear it in coaching session after session: the monthly expenses to sustain everyday life are insane, the cash runway to start a business is nonexistent, and the fear of being laid off is ever-present.

Job loss used to be a private tragedy. And it's not just the money that hurts—it's the psychological whiplash of going from "high performer" to "redundant" overnight. The crushing realization that your value was always conditional, always fragile, always one PowerPoint presentation away from disappearing.

And don't get me started on college education. In 1955, tuition at a public university was $243 a year. That's $2,700 in today's money. You could work a part-time job and pay for your education and your fancy apartment without student loans (like our friend Peggy). Can you imagine?

The GI Bill sent millions of veterans to college. And corporate tax rates were 52%.

Fifty. Two. Percent.

And companies? They actually invested in and protected their workers. Here's a great example of what that looked like in case you are curious: from the Great Depression until the early 1990s, IBM operated under a "full employment" policy. It meant that if your job wasn't needed, you'd be retrained and reassigned to another role. As long as you did your job, you had job security, because the company believed workers performed better when they felt secure, not expendable. Imagine that!

Oh, and CEOs? They made twenty times what the average worker earned.

Not 351 times. Twenty.

But when state funding for education collapsed—starting in the late 1960s under Reagan in California, then accelerating nationwide in the 1980s when he became president—college tuition rates exploded. And now 43 million Americans owe a collective $1.77 trillion for their education. What a fucking trap door.

You know what you *don't* do when you owe $100K in student loans?

Start a business. Take a sabbatical. Have a baby. Or sleep.

My grandfather sent three kids to college. My dad graduated debt-free. Me? I'm just hoping to pay off my MBA degree before my knees give out.

Then there's American healthcare. Or as I like to call it, job jail!

Did you know that in 1960, healthcare cost 4% of your income. Today? It's 18%. That's not insurance. That's a hostage situation, people!

So now we have to stay in soul-crushing jobs to keep our health insurance (unless we want to risk financial ruin over a sinus infection). Cool, cool.

This is what economic precarity looks like in the knowledge economy. It's not a bunch of shuttered factories. It's the slow, suffocating anxiety that no amount of effort will ever be enough to create the life you thought you were working toward.

BETRAYAL #2: INVISIBLE LABOR

The Myth: You have the support system to work full time.

Let me guess. As you are reading this, you are also trying to remember if you scheduled that dentist appointment for your kid and wondering what the hell you're making for dinner tonight.

Can we talk about this for a second?

Because I have a theory: every single job in Corporate America was designed for someone who has a wife at home. Not a partner. Not a co-parent. An agreeable 1950s housewife. With help of her own.

One who magically makes groceries appear, remembers every birthday, rotates the hand towels seasonally to show off to house guests, and somehow never breaks into silent rage while unloading the dishwasher.

And if you *don't* have one of those? Congratulations. You're expected to *be* one—while also crushing those Q3 goals and pretending your child's head lice isn't throwing off your entire week.

She'd also manage all your appointments. The primary doctor visits. That pesky oil change. She knows when your car registration expires and where your passport is.

She's basically your *personal assistant*—except she works for free, and sleeps with you.

The only problem? She's imaginary.

Think about it.

Like I said earlier—the 9-to-5 job structure was built in an era when most households had *split responsibilities*: One person earned the money. The other person handled . . . literally *everything* else.

And guess what? Modern workplaces? They continue to operate like that family system *still exists*.

They expect the same hours, the same availability, the same obsessive devotion—as if someone else is at home, managing your entire *life*.

Don had Betty. You have Google Calendar alerts and a sense of mounting dread.

And the burden of all this? It doesn't fall evenly. It falls—predictably, relentlessly—on women.

Women who somehow manage to hold down full-time careers *and* still do 60% of domestic labor (more, if you count the compounding mental load and emotional triage).

But it's not just women. Single parents juggle impossible schedules with duct tape and caffeine too. Middle-aged adults are sandwiched between caring for their aging parents and their own kids. And disabled workers? They're navigating a workplace that was never designed for them in the first place!

Betrayal #3: Time Theft

The Myth: Work ends when the day does.

My grandfather's workday was a bit different than Don's. No late-night happy hours or affairs for Gordon! When the factory whistle blew, he put down his tools, went home, had dinner with his family, and slept without his boss haunting his dreams like some professional poltergeist.

There was a *boundary*. A line between work and life. A literal factory whistle!

And now?

Now we have Slack. Smartphones. "Flexible" work arrangements—which is just code for *work-from-everywhere-all-the-time.*

Your full-time job has effectively become a needy partner. It lives in your pocket. Interrupts your dinner. And whispers "just circling back on this" out of your Amazon Echo speaker while you're brushing your teeth or showering.

Somehow these technologies collectively have convinced you that if you don't check them constantly, the whole world might collapse.

Microsoft literally coined the term "The Infinite Workday" recently to describe this phenomenon. Messages arriving at all hours with the implicit expectation of immediate response. "Urgent" loses all meaning when everything is urgent. The tools that promised to make work more efficient have instead made work never-ending.

This is *Invasion of the Body Snatchers*, but, like, for your attention span,

Our brains, already fried from information overload, now effectively serve every technology master simultaneously. The result is what researchers call "continuous partial attention"—basically being bad at everything because you're trying to do it all simultaneously.

Remember when you could build expertise through deep focus over time? Those were the days! Now the tools change faster than you can learn them, and there's no time to actually master anything because you're too busy responding to the notification that just lit up your phone screen.

We're not just overworked. We're chronically overstimulated, like hamsters on wheels that are also on fire.

BETRAYAL #4: PERVERSE INCENTIVES

The Myth: Your loyalty will be rewarded.

Once upon a time, sticking with one company meant something. People got perks for that shit. Companies would train their new hires, mentor rising stars, and retain a cohort of professional loyalists who knew where all the metaphorical bodies were buried. Companies invested in those people because those people stuck around. And those people stayed because companies made it worth it.

Not with swag or pizza parties. But with *pensions*.

It was a system built on reciprocity. You give your loyalty, and the company gives a damn.

Now? Stay more than two years and recruiters start squinting like you're hiding a felony.

And the worst part? Studies show that people who stay put earn up to 50% less over their lifetimes than people who bounce every couple of years.

Let me repeat that louder for the company loyalists in the back: Fifty. Percent. Less. OMG.

This isn't an accident. It all comes back to something called fiduciary duty—which sounds noble, like some sort of character from *Downton Abbey*, but is really just corporate legalese for: "maximizing shareholder value" which came into vogue in the 1980s thanks to activist investors like Barry Diller.

This concept has poisoned the entire well of American business.

In theory, it was supposed to keep executives honest.

In practice? It turned American businesses sold on the New York Stock Exchange into giant machines whose gears ran on headcount reductions and stock buybacks. The logic was simple and soulless: buy back stock, juice the stock price, do it again next quarter. Wall Street cheers, executives get bonuses, and the idea of corporate loyalty from the 50s and 60s gets thrown out the window.

Now the executives preaching about culture and engagement are the same ones perpetuating systems that make both impossible. They talk about their employees with care while treating them like equipment—useful until depreciated, then tossed out for a newer model.

And yet we're all supposed to smile through our layoffs, sign the exit paperwork, and thank our employers on Linkedin for the opportunity. Gross.

Betrayal #5: Crisis of Purpose

The Myth: Your work matters.

Walk into any corporate office and you'll see it everywhere. Highly educated people performing elaborate productivity theater. Updating project management software that no one reads, attending meetings about meetings, crafting emails about problems that shouldn't exist in the first place. Everyone's busy—God, are they busy!—but ask them what they actually accomplish in a day, and the answer gets vague real fast.

For most of the 20th century, middle-class knowledge work came with a built-in purpose. You weren't just earning a paycheck—you were building America! Making products people needed, providing services that improved lives, and contributing to an economy you could see growing before your eyes.

That narrative held even when the work sucked. At least it meant something, right?

But today? Today's knowledge workers live in organizations that exist primarily to generate returns for shareholders they'll never meet. Solve problems that mainly exist to justify other departments solving *adjacent* problems in an endless ouroboros loop of institutional nonsense.

Where there were once clear lines between effort and outcome, now there are endless, elaborate metrics that measure everything except whether any of this is worth doing.

We're credentialed beyond belief but feel increasingly irrelevant with AI breathing down our necks.

And our job titles sound impressive until you try to explain them to a child or your retired neighbor. (Try it sometime, I dare you.)

Tell me. What happens if you don't show up tomorrow?

The answer is uncomfortable to face, because it reveals how bastardized modern knowledge work has become.

Meanwhile, companies merge, dissolve, and "pivot" so often that emotionally investing in any of them feels like a form of self-harm.

Why care about a company that might be sold to a private equity firm next quarter?

The result? A uniquely modern form of alienation.

We get elaborate, exhausting activity that consumes massive human energy and produces nothing of lasting value. It's institutional masturbation . . . and we're the lube.

No wonder depression and anxiety are soaring among knowledge workers.

This is why "quiet quitting" became a thing. Why "acting your wage" became a rallying cry. People haven't given up on work. They've seen through the fantasy that corporate work matters.

And you know what? This crisis of purpose? It's not fixable with better perks, kombucha-on-tap, or an ERG for women and POCs.

What we feel is structural and spiritual. If work doesn't connect to a purpose, if the brightest minds spend their lives optimizing ad algorithms and designing subscription cancellation flows that trap people in services they don't want, we've built an economy that's actively harmful to humanity.

So if you're sitting there wondering why your important-sounding job feels completely meaningless? If you're questioning whether any of this matters?

You're not crazy. Or ungrateful. You're just waking up to wanting more.

BETRAYAL #6: SELF-CENSURE

The Myth: Success means fitting in.

This one is so subtle, so sneaky, you don't even notice it happening.

Until one day you catch your own reflection—in the microwave door of the kitchen, in a Zoom window, or in the too-bright bathroom mirror at 6:48 AM—and think: *Who the hell even is that?*

Corporate America doesn't just want your time. It wants your edges. Your spark. Your weirdness. Your inconvenient curiosity.

It needs you to become: . . . Less interesting. Less opinionated. Less alive. Don't rock the boat, baby.

Interesting people rock the boat.

They ask questions.

They suggest better ways to do things.

That's messy. And messy isn't governable.

You learn, instead, to be a "team player." To smile in meetings even when your soul is actively leaving your body. You begrudgingly go along with it all.

Because everyone else is doing it. And before you know it, you're in khakis and a branded fleece, nodding earnestly on a call about cross-functional alignment, with no idea how you got here.

You've become a derivative of Trish from HR.

You slowly hide the parts of yourself that don't fit neatly into the org chart. Suppress the interests that live outside your job description. You pretend—subtly, skillfully, over time—that the complex, contradictory, evolving human you actually *are* is somehow less valuable than the one-dimensional professional persona you've learned to perform.

And beneath that polished veneer, something devastating happens.

You start to erase the very parts of yourself that made you creative. That made you interesting. That made you, well, *you*.

The psychological cost of this is impossible to quantify but painfully easy to spot: it shows up in the careful blankness on people's faces when asked a real question at work. The studied conversational neutrality any time a spicy topic comes up.

You didn't start out your career in corporate this way. You weren't *born* boring. You didn't *want* to be safe and small. You've just internalized corporate predictability so thoroughly, you sort of forgot who you were before the lanyard.

We get elaborate, exhausting activity that consumes massive human energy and produces nothing of lasting value. It's institutional masturbation ... and we're the lube.

Look, the postwar middle-class boom was perhaps the biggest socioeconomic experiment in U.S. history. If you are not Gen Z, you have memories of when things didn't feel so flipping hard. Which means you are sort of clinging to this sense of nostalgia: of what white middle-class American knowledge work *should* look and feel like.

So if you found yourself nodding along to everything you read in this chapter, let me break it down for you:

If one or two of those betrayals from this chapter hit home, welcome to having a job in Corporate America! It can stink sometimes, but that's called adult life. Like eating airplane food or making small talk with your dentist. Not every day is going to be a cakewalk but sometimes you have to tolerate some shit.

If three or four of these betrayals made you go "OH MY GOD, YES," then honey, you're dealing with some serious problems that no amount of positive thinking or therapy can fix.

You can't yoga your way out of feeling the way you do.

And if FIVE or even ALL SIX of these betrayals made you feel personally attacked by reality?

Listen to me carefully: It is time for a change!

I say this with all the gentleness in my heart: It's time to choose yourself instead of a company that doesn't give a shit about you.

Cuz let's be honest—Don Draper wasn't real anyways. He was completely made up. A figment of the American imagination. A beautifully tortured, chain-smoking metaphor for everything we were promised and will never get.

Clearly, I love watching *Mad Men*, but maybe it's time for us to change the damn channel.

WAYFINDING

CHAPTER FOUR

THE PERSONAL BRAND INDUSTRIAL COMPLEX

April 2024

Earlier today, I had filed the business paperwork, paid the $200 licensing fee, and—*jazz hands*—officially became a founder!

And yet, there I was, awake at 3 a.m., my face pressed against the cold black tile of the master bathroom floor, whispering "I can't do this!" into the void like a deranged Victorian heroine.

My husband is sitting next to me on the floor, quietly holding my hand for comfort. He doesn't say anything, because what could he say? He just sits in solidarity while I hyperventilate about my unemployment benefits, business coaching invoices, and whether my LinkedIn headline is cringe.

(It is. It absolutely is.)

In addition to starting a business, I've also tried to slough off my grief by becoming, in short, a kind of corporate mystic. Bullet journaling my way to enlightenment and another W-2.

And when none of that worked? I went nuclear.

I told myself starting a business was a triumph. A brave new chapter! In reality, it was a Hail Mary pass, and I'd completely lost the plot.

And so began my entrepreneurial wanderabout. The season where I was convinced the answer wasn't crawling back to Corporate America, but striking out on my own.

When I first launched my coaching practice, it felt electric.

I did it because I had missed helping people. I longed for those one-on-one conversations problem solving with colleagues. I missed the camaraderie of building something with other people. Coaching gave me a new version of that energy. And I knew I'd be good at it!

It was exhilarating to channel my product and marketing skills into something wholly mine. I learned new things, too: website development, sales, copywriting, SEO (which I found weirdly thrilling). I loved that every experiment, every conversation, and every tiny iteration of the process was mine to claim.

And I will never forget the feeling of closing my first paying client. The rush was like oxygen—a tiny proof point that, maybe, just maybe, I could sustain myself on my own ideas and services. After years of building products in support of other people's visions, here was something different: my own vision.

It was terrifying. But it also felt very alive.

There were days when I would walk away from a coaching call buzzing—literally buzzing—like my nervous system had been plugged into a clean socket. I had forgotten what it was like to end a day feeling like I had delivered something of value.

Even the unglamorous parts carried their own charge. Wrestling with Squarespace. Teaching myself how to set up a Stripe account. Writing my first sales page, equal parts awkward and proud. These weren't chores; they were initiations! Each one seemed to whisper to me, "You are capable of more than you think."

For all its hardships, entrepreneurship had a heartbeat.

But, fun fact, you don't magically transform into a different person the moment you create an LLC.

All those toxic patterns that made you want to fake your own death to escape corporate life? Congratulations! They're coming with you to your shiny new business venture like the world's worst housewarming gift. The perfectionism, the people-pleasing, the inability to set boundaries, the compulsive need to prove you're not a fraud—it all transfers over with the efficiency of the coronavirus.

This sucks for obvious reasons, but here's what makes it extra sucky: most of us jump into the land of entrepreneurship as an escape hatch. We're running FROM something (usually a boss we wanted to throat-punch) rather than running TO something. Classic fight or flight. But when you're in full sprint mode, you don't exactly have time to examine the belief systems and terrible habits that got you into this existential mess in the first place.

I figured this out the hard way when I caught myself checking email on a Saturday during a date with my husband. He very gently pointed out that this was happening, and he was 100% right for calling it out. Nobody was making me do that. I didn't have some micromanaging boss breathing down my neck. I was choosing to ruin my own weekend because I couldn't bear the thought of a client thinking I was unprofessional or—God forbid—unreliable.

The only difference between my old job and my new "freedom" was that now I couldn't blame anyone else for the pattern. It was just me, myself, and my deeply internalized capitalism—hanging out together in my home office while I slowly lost my mind trying to drum up new clients.

I need to acknowledge something here before we continue: I had access to important sources of privilege, including the gift of some money and, therefore, time. I had zero incentive to crawl right back to Corporate America just yet, even though my ego occasionally tried to submit my résumé behind my back.

But let the record show that I also didn't take months and months off just resting and healing.

I jumped right into the entrepreneurship thing. Like I was auditioning for Shark Tank.

I mean, I thought I was doing all the "self-care" stuff too—meditation apps, loads of therapy, I even bought an expensive candle that was supposed to represent "new beginnings." But grief, despite my pushiness, was working on its own (verrrrrry slow) schedule.

I wish I had given myself more time off. I really, really do. I probably wouldn't have had that aforementioned panic attack.

The only upside to that whole bathroom situation is that I can now spot, with terrifying accuracy, when a prospective client is absolutely not ready for coaching. Or starting a business. Or whatever it is they think will save them from actually feeling their feelings.

I see it now on discovery calls—that subtle panic disguised as hyper-productivity, the nervous laughter, and the frantic need for a plan.

And when I see this, I want to say: "Babe. You don't need a marketing plan. You need a nap and a good bloodcurdling scream into a pillow."

Sometimes the first step after leaving a job isn't to jump to the next thing. It's to slow down enough to realize that your nervous system is still on fire, and that no, you can't hack your way back to happiness if your body still thinks that it's under siege.

Trust me. I've tried to spreadsheet my way out of this shit. It does not work.

You can't avoid rock bottom. Instead, those feelings you're avoiding? They become your constant companions. Your full-time co-workers, even. And they start to outnumber you.

Jumping ship from corporate, I quickly learned, was more like . . . jumping into a different ocean—with more waves. Sharks too! And no lifeguard.

It was just me, myself, and my deeply internalized capitalism—hanging out together in my home office while I slowly lost my mind trying to drum up new clients.

In fact, online entrepreneurship requires a specific kind of resilience that nobody warns you about. You get bombarded with a nonstop feed of curated success stories. Six-figure months. Seven-figure launches. TikToks with soothing audio and text overlays like: "Here's how I built my dream life in six easy steps!"

And meanwhile you're over here like: I built a website with Squarespace and cried into my sandwich today, would you look at me?

There's very little consistent external validation in the beginning, unless you are lucky. There's no manager telling you once a week that you're crushing it. No awkward kitchen chats by the microwave over bad coffee. No trauma-bonded colleagues to whom you can whisper "I hate this, too!"

It's just you in the beginning. You, your laptop, your new-business anxiety, and that ever-growing pile of business books that all seem to contradict each other. But you keep showing up anyway—not because you're sure it'll work, but because something in you refuses to quit.

Then there's the financial reality: If you don't have a gigantic cash runway—and let's be honest, most of us do not—you have to take whatever clients you can get in the beginning.

Which means you might have to sacrifice what you actually value. Your time and/or your principles.

You might, for example, find yourself on Zoom with a prospective client who gives you a stress rash. But you smile and nod and say things like, "Amazing insight, I'd love to work together!" while silently dissociating on camera.

The tradeoffs are real and they're vicious. Without enough savings, you can't afford to be picky about clients.

Without enough clients, you can't afford to set boundaries. Without enough boundaries, you burn out faster than that regrettable candle in your bedroom.

The really messed up part? Money doesn't fix these patterns either. Over the past two and a half years, I have watched multiple entrepreneurs—and these are smart people with multiple six-figure businesses—have very public meltdowns on social media. Like, the kind where you're reading their Instagram stories thinking, *"Should someone ask them if they're okay?"*

Last month, someone I follow on Substack—who regularly posts about her media empire—shared that she'd been hospitalized for physical exhaustion. Another entrepreneur I know—who speaks at conferences and has a podcast—admitted to me over drinks that she takes anti-anxiety medication because the pressure to maintain her success trajectory is too much to bear at times.

These are people who have "made it" by every traditional vanity metric (hundreds of thousands of social followers and self-sustaining incomes) and are also still being destroyed by the systems they've created for themselves. They escaped Corporate America only to re-create a mini version of it in their own venture.

Then there is the little fact that you are likely a team of one which means you can't call in sick when you're the CEO, the marketing department, AND the secretary whose job it is to report your illness to everyone you have a meeting with today. You can't take mental health days when your income depends on you showing up with a smile and a can-do attitude. You can't set boundaries when every "no" potentially costs you next month's rent.

It's sad, right? We escape corporate jobs because we're tired of being treated like revenue-generating machines, then we start businesses where we treat ourselves like . . . revenue-generating machines. We leave positions where our worth was measured by output, then we create companies where our worth is measured by . . . wait for it . . . output!

Money! Growth! Productivity! Scale! More, bigger, faster, better, until you die!

So where does that leave us?

Corporate employment will slowly kill your soul, one status meeting at a time. And traditional entrepreneurship? Without bumper guards? It'll chew you up and spit you out too.

I know what you're thinking: "Wow, Brie, kill the vibe why don't you. Really glad I bought this feel-good career book."

Look—I'm not saying entrepreneurship is bad. (I absolutely love being an entrepreneur.) And I'm definitely not suggesting we all go quietly back to our open-office hellboxes.

What I am saying is this: Jumping from a broken system without examining what broke you in the first place isn't liberation. It's just changing the color of your prison jumpsuit. It's still polyester and it's still going to chafe your thigh gap, okay?

So when I look back at that 3 a.m. moment on the bathroom floor—the unpaid invoices, the spiritual bypassing, the bone-deep exhaustion—I see it with more compassion now.

It was at that moment when I decided I had to redefine what "enough" meant to me—and, in doing so, rediscover what it meant to build a body of work on my terms.

That, I thought, was where true freedom lived.

CHAPTER FIVE

PORTFOLIO CAREER CURIOUS

May 2024

I'm at yet another entrepreneur mixer with name tags, overpriced wine, and shit tons of humility cosplay.

I'm watching this boisterous Norman with a mullet explain how he scaled his passion for wellness into an influencer brand.

Everyone's nodding like he's just cracked cold fusion; which is odd to me because he just sells protein powder to gym bros on Tiktok.

Then it happens. He turns to me and asks me the following question, "So, what do YOU do?"

I hate this question. I viscerally hate this question.

Panicked, I vomit word salad.

"Well, I do some coaching . . . and I write . . . and I help people with marketing strategy . . . and I run workshops . . . uh, sometimes?"

Not the fucking uptalk! Why did my voice go up at the end like I'm asking HIM what I do for work?

"Oh!" he says, like I've just solved climate change. "You have a portfolio career!"

A what? Is that what the kids are calling what I'm doing?

Jonesing to solve this mystery, I rush off to a corner to Google this term.

Oh my GOD. This is it!

"The portfolio career," I say wittily in my best impersonation of David Attenborough to my friend via voice note later that evening as I walk home.

In the vast, unpredictable ecosystem of the modern economy, a curious creature has begun to emerge—adaptable, elusive, and resistant to traditional classification.

Behold... the Portfolio Careerist!

Unlike its more predictable cousin, the Nine-to-Fiver, this species of working professional cannot be found in just one habitat. Instead, it flits between environments—freelance projects, consulting gigs, creative ventures, and perhaps a podcast or two—all coexisting in a delicate, ever-evolving balance.

Observe how it forages for income streams across various disciplines, assembling a patchwork of roles that defies the rigid confines of a job title. Its survival depends not on stability, but on diversification—a trait honed by necessity and ambition alike.

While some traditionalists may view its lack of a singular focus with suspicion, make no mistake: this creature is not lost. It is exploring! Thriving. Redefining what it means to work, one Slack notification and Google Document at a time.

And as the climate of employment continues to shift, we may find that this once-rare creature is not just surviving . . . but quietly leading the way toward a new collective future!"

I hit send.

My friend immediately texts back: "You're such a weirdo, you know that right?"

That night, energized by my new discovery and probably too much wine, I did something that would prove to be more revelatory than several months of therapy, meditation, and those expensive business books combined. I sat cross-legged on my living room floor (That position always demands radical honesty, doesn't it?) and started documenting what I had actually been doing for the past five months.

The task started innocently enough.

I listed the obvious billable stuff:

- Coaching clients: 15 hours-per-week

- Marketing consulting: 10 hours-per-week

- Workshop prep and facilitation: 5 hours-per-week

Thirty hours. Respectable!

But my pen, having developed a mind of its own, kept moving across the page like it was possessed by the ghost of productivity past.

There were . . . other things too:

- Managing family caregiving including an insurance nightmare: 6 hours-per-week

- Volunteer work with the local housing nonprofit: 4 hours-per-week

- Learning new skills—AI tools, podcast editing, whatever seemed essential to not becoming obsolete as a tech professional: 3 hours-per-week

- Therapy and exercise: 4 hours-per-week

- Creative projects of undetermined merit: 3 hours-per-week

I put down my pen and stared at this list.

Fifty hours of intentional work each week. A whole portfolio! Nearly six full workdays of work. And yet, in all my shame-filled networking conversations, I had only been comfortable discussing the shit that I was paid for.

I had been trying to compress an entire novel of labor into a 140-character tweet. No wonder I felt scattered. No wonder "What do you do?" set off the mental panic button. I had all of these other things that were desiring to be accounted for and known by the world.

For the first time in months, my shoulders dropped from their permanent residence around my ears. My jaw—chronically clenched with the effort of appearing competent—finally relaxed.

I wasn't failing at focus. I wasn't constitutionally incapable of professional commitment. No, no! I was a human being whose life had achieved something that had somehow eluded me for forty-one years of life: actual, honest-to-God integration.

Are we ALL portfolio careerists? I wondered.

It sure feels like it, doesn't it? Everyone seems to have side hustles these days just to stay afloat.

But as I thought more about it in that particular moment, I realized the answer was *no*.

Most of us—myself included—weren't yet portfolio careerists.

We were *polyworkers*.

Polywork, or at least how I reasoned it, sat right in the middle between gig work and a true portfolio career. Let me explain.

THE CREATIVE
AUTONOMY CURVE

Gig Work

Trading time for money.
- **Motivation:** Cash and/or flexibility.
- **Operating system**: Capitalism. (womp, womp.)

Polywork

Managing multiple roles/projects at once.
- **Motivations:** Income optionality. Financial protection. Work-life integration.
- **Operating system:** Your values + capitalism's.

Portfolio Career

The nirvana state of polyworking. Designing a self-directed body of work.
- **Motivations:** Creative freedom, purpose, working on your terms.
- **Operating system:** Your value system!

Want FREE digital copies of the Polyworker frameworks?

Scan this QR code to download now.

Gig work is when you trade time for money, renting your skills to pay your bills. Whether you're clocking in for a 9-to-5, freelancing between clients, or delivering DoorDash orders, the mechanics are the same. You give your hours in exchange for a wage, and the value you create flows upward, bolstering someone else's bottom line. (Unless, of course, you're one of the lucky few who receive stock options–in which case, carry on.)

To be clear, there's dignity in this kind of work. It pays the bills, feeds your family, and even gives you a sense of belonging or purpose if you're lucky. But in a post-AI economy, over-indexing on gig work comes with risk. When your stability depends entirely on what I call your anchor income, you're exposed to forces beyond your control–job automation, policy shifts, economic mood swings–more than you'd ever choose to be.

If your job or contract disappears, so does your safety net! And if you've been too busy surviving to build assets or a network, there's no cushion when the bottom falls out from under you.

Then there's another kind of pressure–the creative kind. That itch you can't quite scratch. The stability your primary income provides might keep you financially afloat, but being creative is what keeps your soul alive. And when your anchor income leaves no room to stretch your skills or do the ballsy things you want to, that same safety net starts to feel like a chokehold. For ambitious, creative people, that kind of stillness can feel like purgatory.

Polywork is a response to the conditions of modern gig work—and a quiet, emerging movement reshaping the very nature of work.

This phenomenon has been most visible in the tech world: a reckoning born in the aftermath of COVID, the rise of AI, and the waves of layoffs that followed a 2022 hiring glut. Together, these forces have compelled many working professionals to reimagine not only how they work, but also for whom they work.

What may start as a practice in financial survival becomes something far deeper—a practice in intuition, autonomy, and creative experimentation. You start stacking roles, projects, and pursuits that match your life circumstances. Maybe that means taking on a fractional marketing role while building a course or launching an Etsy shop to sell your handmade ceramics. Whatever form it takes, polywork is about reclaiming agency, a bit of income insurance, and a sense of control.

As a polyworker, you're actively seeking work that aligns with your values, attempting to set boundaries (however porous they sometimes feel), and experimenting with what might be possible for your career. It's liberating and disorienting in equal measure. And those internal scripts? The ones that whisper what you should want? They, unfortunately, still hijack your career's operating system from time to time. (I know, I know—such a sonofabitch!)

That's because you're in transition—actively retraining your nervous system to believe you can design your career on your own terms and rebuilding your self-trust to know that you alone define what success looks like in this model of work.

Polywork, in this light, is both a creative act and a proving ground—a delicate choreography between stability and freedom. Some days it feels like improvisation; other days, it feels like you've finally found the beat. And while it's not yet the full expression of a portfolio career, it's the bridge that makes one possible—the collective practice that's helping future generations of workers cross the chasm to creative sovereignty too!

A Portfolio Career is like the nirvana state of polyworking. As a portfolio careerist, you've become creatively ungovernable, because you've begun building evidence of your own value apart from your anchor income. You've replaced traditional employment contracts with new creative covenants—with your values, your energy, and your craft. It's a complete reset of your professional operating system, one that de-centers those aforementioned internal scripts and re-architects your career around a larger purpose and your zone of genius.

Here, your labor becomes an expression of your human design, interests, and limits. In this stage of creative autonomy, your body of work becomes an act of devotion. Your anchor income hums quietly in the background, but your owned portfolio—your self-authored body of work—is what accrues the real interest. It's what builds wealth, not just for you, but for the people and projects you care about most.

Zoom out far enough, and you'll see it oh so clearly: The polyworker movement is what makes the portfolio career era of work possible. We are a constellation of workers lighting the path toward a new way forward, proving that work was never meant to follow a single script!

Of course, I recognize that not everyone will want—or be able to afford—to live and work this way. They may even think it's bananas! It's also worth noting that a portfolio career can come with different pressures: an expectation to constantly monetize your skills or to turn everything into a product or a social post. The line between self-expression and self-exploitation is razor thin.

I acknowledge all of the above. But I still don't think it invalidates the model or the philosophy behind it. If anything, it humanizes it—and reinforces why I describe autonomy as a continuum. Creative sovereignty isn't a permanent state; it's a practice. We will all oscillate between polyworking and portfolio-careering mode, sometimes daily, depending on our unique context.

When I consciously chose to graduate from the land of polywork to a portfolio career, the road didn't get easier, but it got a hell of a lot clearer. My north star sharpened into focus as the big question guiding my day-to-day decisions shifted from, "How do I survive this?" to "What exactly am I building toward?" It prompted me to honor my own experience and desires and, as such, make different choices when I was no longer sleepwalking my way through my career.

I became so passionate about it, I eventually started teaching other people how to build their own creative empire too.

The polyworker movement is what makes the portfolio career era of work possible. We are a constellation of workers lighting the path toward a new way forward, proving that work was never meant to follow a single script!

CHAPTER SIX

CHARLES HANDY SAW THIS COMING

June 2024

Once I'd discovered the #PortfolioCareerLife, I spent time researching the career model and stumbled across this soulful Irish org management thinker named Charles Handy.

Charles Handy. Even his name sounds like someone who'd have all the answers, doesn't it? Like he'd fix your leaky faucet and then explain the meaning of life over tea.

I was immediately obsessed.

Turns out, Charles coined this term "portfolio career" back in the '80s. The actual '80s. While everyone else was doing cocaine and donning shoulder pads, this man was quietly authoring a movement.

You know that feeling when you realize you're not the first person to have a thought? That sort of professional communion where you say to yourself, "*Oh goodie, I'm NOT completely unhinged?*"

This was one of those moments, and I felt deeply comforted.

His story was incredible. He'd been a higher up at Shell—Shell! The oil company!—and then just woke up one day, said "nope," and wandered off to become a university professor, a consultant, a writer, and then—wait for it—Warden of Windsor Castle.

But what really sucked me in wasn't his résumé. It was this radical idea of his—way ahead of its time—that work should serve our humanity instead of swallowing it whole.

Revolutionary concept. Almost like we're humans first and productivity machines second.

Wild.

So naturally, I read everything that Google would give me for free, and by morning I'd ordered three of his books from Amazon with overnight shipping.

This gentle London Business School professor had somehow prophesied where late-stage capitalism was heading thirty years before the rest of us caught on. While Gordon Gekko was declaring "greed is good," Sir Handy was quietly mapping out an alternative way of working for all of us.

In the days that followed, his frameworks gave me concrete language for the things I had been stewing over privately. He saw the death of the traditional career ladder—predicted the outsourcing, the downsizing—long before the internet and the gig economy even existed.

I was not crazy. We were not crazy.

Armed with this newfound philosophy, I went full mad scientist mode on my coaching clients. I started talking to them about Handy's ideas and this concept of a self-authored career architecture.

But then I would inevitably get these blank stares back, and statements like, "Well, what do you mean?"

Handy's original framework, brilliant as it was, was too conceptual. And it was built for a different era—before the gig economy atomized stable work and before eldercare and childcare collided in real-time with trying to finish a client proposal from our home offices.

My clients couldn't do much with his manifesto. They needed a framework!

That's when I remembered the Business Model Canvas. Introduced in the late 2000s, this one-page framework transformed startup planning. Rather than wrestling with dense 40-page business plans filled with financial models and market research, founders could focus on the essential building blocks of their startup venture: their value proposition, customer segments, their revenue model, and key partnerships.

I thought it would be pretty cool to apply that same one-page approach to career planning. So I took Charles Handy's portfolio career philosophy, updated it to reflect modern workplace realities and gender equity considerations, and distilled it down to a one page framework.

Great success!

The canvas format resonated with my clients because it made the abstract tangible. Instead of getting lost in endless reflection, they now had a one-page tool to map out how different forms of their labor could work together and support the life they wanted to create. They could take risks, spot resource gaps, and adjust their approach to building a portfolio career for their unique context—all before making major commitments.

THE PORTFOLIO CAREER CANVAS

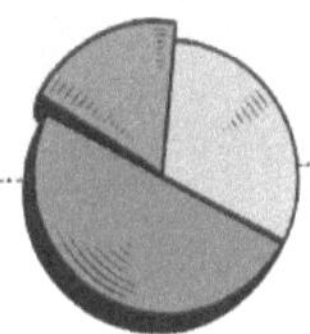

Wage Work

Meaningful paid roles where you contribute your skills and time in exchange for a W-2 salary or freelance or fractional wage.

Acts of Service

Work you do to give back to the world and your community at large, often driven by a deep sense of purpose or values rather than compensation.

Experiments

Entrepreneurial or freelance work where you set your own rates and terms. Economic viability, profitability & your general interest level TBD.

Caregiving

The "unseen" infrastructure of society. Unpaid labor within families and communities — emotional support, coordination, and practical care that make all other work possible.

Upskilling

Intentional learning and professional development activities that expand your existing capabilities and hard + soft skill sets.

Self Care

This is the space you protect to care for your own wellbeing including your physical, spiritual, and mental health.

Want FREE digital copies of the Polyworker frameworks?

Scan this QR code to download now.

The Portfolio Career Canvas

Your portfolio essentially consists of 6 forms of labor at all times:

- Wage Work

- Caregiving

- Acts of Service

- Upskilling

- Experiments

- Self-Care

Your Wage Work

Definition: The stuff that pays your bills.

Examples: Full-time jobs, fractional consulting and/or recurring freelance work. These are your predictable income streams. They provide stability and, if you are lucky, benefits.

But be careful. Wage work is greedy. It will consume every available hour and brain cell, creeping into your evenings and your weekends. The key is to treat this portion of your portfolio as *one* component. Not the whole show!

Questions to ask yourself:

- Is this work energizing or draining me?

- What am I actually gaining from doing this? (Besides money, obviously.)

- How much of my identity is wrapped up in this particular form of work?

- What boundaries do I need to create to protect time for other forms of my labor?

Your Caregiving

Definition: Unpaid labor that keeps the people you love functioning.

Examples: Childcare, eldercare, supporting a partner through challenges, being that friend that people call when they're in crisis, managing family logistics.

This work rarely shows up on our résumés, but it's often the most important work we do.

It is important to *value this work* even if capitalism doesn't. And to actually negotiate the terms of this work with the other people in your household. I'm giving you permission right now to remind your spouse/partner/sibling that they need to pick up the slack. Take out the trash. Clean those dirty dishes in the sink. (Or remember to call their mother once in a while!)

Questions to ask yourself:

- What skills am I developing through my caregiving?

- Do I need help?

- If I do, who could share this load with me, so I don't combust?

- How can I honor and celebrate this work with others?

Your Acts of Service

Definition: Unpaid labor; typically "give back" projects within your chosen communities.

Examples: Mentoring, volunteering, organizing community events, advocacy work, serving on boards.

This work is deeply identity-affirming. It reminds you who you are beyond your wage work and connects you to something larger than yourself. It's often where you get to use soft skills that your wage work may not tap into as regularly.

Also, acts of service build better networks! When you show up consistently for causes you care about, you meet people who share your values who can vouch for you.

Questions to ask yourself:

- How can I contribute to my communities of choice in ways that leverage my unique strengths?

- How (if at all) does this form of labor feed my soul?

- How can participation in my community be a source of energy and inspiration in my life?

Your Upskilling

Definition: Intentional learning that builds capabilities for future opportunities.

Examples: Taking courses or an improv class, reading industry books, experimenting with AI tools, attending conferences, getting certifications, learning new software.

Most people treat learning like a nice-to-have. Given the pace of change today, continuous skill-building is mission-critical. The half-life of skills is shrinking every damn day! What got you here won't get you *there*. All those clichés are annoyingly true.

Questions to ask yourself:

- What skills do I need to develop to get where I want to be in two years?

- How can I make learning a regular habit instead of something I squeeze in when I can?

- What's my natural learning style, and am I actually honoring it?

Your Experiments

Definition: Messy, highly uncertain, early-stage ideas that *may or may not* become something bigger.

Examples: Launching a newsletter for fun, testing a product prototype.

This work rarely has clear outcomes or timelines, which can make them feel indulgent or like a wasteful investment. But, make sure to create space for your own creative laboratory, if you will. Think of your experiments like two-way doors—you can always walk away if they don't work out or feel right. But they cultivate your sense of play and childlike wonder.

Questions to ask yourself:

- What ideas have I been carrying around that deserve exploration?

- What would I attempt if I knew I couldn't fail?

Your Self Care

Definition: Intentional effort to sustain your mental, emotional, and physical capacity.

Examples: Therapy, exercise, meditation, adequate sleep, time off, spiritual practices.

You are the vessel through which all labor flows. When you're completely depleted, nothing else works. Not your job. Not your relationships. Not your experiments.

When you think of it this way, rest isn't selfish. It's strategic! (And P.S. Self-care isn't just bubble baths and face masks. It's more like understanding your own recovery rhythms and working *with* them instead of against them.)

Questions to ask yourself:

- Where do I need stronger boundaries to protect my wellbeing?

- How can I build restoration into my daily routine?

- Are there seasons of the year where I need to build in downtime to recharge my batteries?

- Am I receiving the full benefits of this form of care or depriving myself of them?

You're looking at this framework now, aren't you? Mentally cataloging everything while thinking to yourself, "Okay cool, but this is actually a big mindset change to commit to." And then another panicky thought might creep in: "How the hell am I going to do this?"

At that moment in my own career transition, I didn't have good answers to these questions. Because I was asking myself the exact same things.

I had the fancy framework, sure. But I, too, was still new to this portfolio career thing at this point in my journey, hobbling along. Barely. With no real accountability, operating system, or psychic boundaries. Nope, I was just making it up as I went along and hoping that no one noticed when I was breaking my own rules.

And every time a client would ask me, "But . . . like, how?" I'd feel that uncomfortable squeeze in my chest. Because I knew what they were really asking. They were asking if it was possible to work this way. If this whole thing was just another pipe dream. If they'd still end up as a one-person sweatshop, just with new-agey vocabulary.

I still needed to figure out how to hold myself accountable before I could teach other people to do the same. Otherwise, I was just a hypocrite with a really nice framework. (And nobody needed another one of those.)

BUILDING

CHAPTER SEVEN

IT'S LONELY IN THIS TOILET STALL

August 2024

I'm standing in a Zoom queue. Not, like, metaphorically. Literally standing in my kitchen in a bright orange blouse that seemed like a good idea until I looked in the mirror. But now it's too late to change, and I look like a human creamsicle, waiting to be let into a virtual workshop to talk about building a portfolio career.

What the hell do I know about building a portfolio career? Why are people looking at ME like I have a clue what I am talking about when I just started to do this two months ago?

Anyway. I do the talk.

Somehow, I don't intellectually brown out. People nod. I even get one of those tiny celebratory reactions from someone on the call who has self-identified as a "fangirl." (What??? I have fan . . . people now?)

Afterward, I'm bracing for the classic, "Thanks so much!" and everyone dropping off the call, as is standard for these sorts of things.

But the CEO that hired me to do the webinar stays on the call to chat.

I immediately assume I've said something wildly inappropriate and am about to be gently reprimanded.

Instead, she thanks me for my presentation, beaming with enthusiasm.

I nod awkwardly, contorting my mouth into a forced smile.

She wants to introduce me to some woman in Australia who "has a similar story."

Cue shock.

Fast forward a few days. I'm on Zoom with the woman I've been introduced to who is absurdly kind. Like . . . *really kind*. Not the Corporate girl boss, tight-smile, "Let me know how I can support you (I won't)" kind. She actually listens. She asks weirdly insightful questions that make me feel both seen *and* slightly vulnerable. In a good way. Maybe.

And then—get this—she offers me resources. Sends a Google doc link in the chat. Introduces me to two people via whatsapp while we're still talking. Suddenly I'm agreeing to virtual coffee next week to discuss my coaching framework. (Which, full disclosure, is held together by duct tape and hope.)

I hang up feeling . . . lighter? Hopeful, even?

Very suspicious.

This doesn't happen in my world. In twenty years of professional networking, this sort of exchange has always been transactional.

So naturally, I'm spiraling. What's the catch? When's the upsell? Is this an MLM? Am I about to be invited to Bali to cry in circles and sell essential oils?

———————

Everyone warns you that entrepreneurship is lonely. But what no one tells you is that portfolio careers are a whole different kind of lonely.

Like, Lindsay Lohan eating her lunch on a toilet in *Mean Girls* lonely.

Traditional employees have colleagues, people they can work on projects with and kvetch about work to.

Entrepreneurs have clubs. Meetups. Books with titles like *The Lean Startup* and *The 4-Hour Workweek*. There's an entire cultural mythology around "being your own boss" that makes it seem sexy and brave.

But portfolio careerists? We're professional pioneers that people don't quite know what to do with yet.

Your family and friends don't understand what you're doing. Like at all.

And you—brilliant, competent, wildly capable person that you are—start to wonder if maybe everyone else is right. Maybe this style of work is, in fact, insane.

The only thing that kept me in it was finding what Leslie Zaikis and Kaylin Aarts of the New HQ call your "chosen colleagues."

The trajectory of my portfolio career really took off after speaking in front of that particular community.

That CEO–the one who hired me to speak–got me. Like, *really* got me. She understood exactly what I was trying to do. And then she helped me by introducing me to her own network, shared resources freely, and checked in month after month without asking for anything in return.

Slowly, I started to realize what I'd been missing all these years of my career.

You see, this CEO's world operated on abundance. Helping another woman succeed didn't mean less success for her. There was enough opportunity, enough clients, enough recognition to go around. We weren't fighting for slices of the same pie–we were baking a bigger one together.

Through her, I met others like me.

There was Sarah, who left law to become a consultant, yoga instructor, and criminal justice reform advocate. Marcus, who somehow balanced freelance design work with coaching Little League and managing his family's Airbnb properties. And Elena, who built tiny houses by day and sold jewelry at weekend markets in Portland.

This new form of professional kinship was evidence of a new order taking shape in the world of work, and a gentle reminder that:

- Real community isn't about networking. It's about *connection* (The kind that doesn't need a calendar invite or an agenda to matter!).

- You can protect space for all your parts. A portfolio career gives you the flexibility to protect space for your entire labor "canvas"—as a wage worker, a parent, tinkerer, and friend. We prove that earning a living and preserving your well-being, creativity, and integrity aren't mutually exclusive. With commitment and accountability, they can, in fact, coexist.

- Scarcity is learned. So is abundance. Traditional employment has taught many of us, especially women, to believe there's only room for a few of us at the big kid table. That belief system turns work into a relentless competition (Ew!). The portfolio career community upends that script. Here, professional relationships become symbiotic, like nature itself—evidence that when we share knowledge, opportunity, and support, *everyone* benefits.

My method for finding my "chosen colleagues" is uniquely mine. If I could offer one piece of advice for finding yours, it's this: Pay attention to who energizes you the first time you meet them. You'll recognize your people by how they make you feel: a little lighter and a little more like yourself. Stick with that process long enough, and one day you'll look up and realize you're not standing alone in that metaphorical toilet stall anymore.

In the late nineteenth century, as industrialization reshaped American life, workers faced a choice—accept the terms set by the Carnegies and Rockefellers or organize. They chose the latter. That particular labor movement didn't just earn people better wages; it fundamentally changed how labor related to power. It proved that when ordinary people organize around shared purpose, they can rewrite the rules embedded in the social contract itself.

There's a reason I keep harping on the importance of finding community in those early stages of polyworking your way toward a portfolio career: The community is what makes this whole model possible.

History has shown us—again and again—that moments of technological change are also moments of political possibility. Take a recent example: In the late nineteenth century, as industrialization reshaped American life, workers faced a choice—accept the terms set by the Carnegies and Rockefellers or organize. They chose the latter. That particular labor movement didn't just earn people better wages; it fundamentally changed how labor related to power. It proved that when ordinary people organize around shared purpose, they can rewrite the rules embedded in the social contract itself.

We're living through a similar inflection point today. The tools are obviously different—we've got AI instead of steel mills and Zoom rooms instead of factory floors—but the question is the same: Who gets to dictate the terms of how we work?

We do.

And *that* is why I get loud about portfolio careers and community building. This movement represents something much bigger than creating more optionality for yourself or working on your terms. It's a rebellion against a set of broken systems that treat human beings like dog doo-doo. I don't know about you, but I'm tired of choosing between my financial security and my dignity. And tired of systems that profit—quite literally—from keeping us desperate, isolated, and afraid.

So the next time you help a fellow portfolio careerist—or a polyworker, for that matter—figure out their pricing model or share a client lead, remember: That simple act of generosity is what keeps the whole ecosystem going. Community isn't an accessory to the portfolio career movement; it's the engine that turns independence into interdependence.

The truth is, the powerful have always known something the rest of us have forgotten:

The more of us who build sustainable, self-authored careers, the weaker those outdated, shitty systems become—and the more space we create for something better to take their place.

Go find your people and build something already. Be dangerous (in the most generous way possible!).

The more of us who build sustainable, self-authored careers, the weaker those outdated, shitty systems become—and the more space we create for something better to take their place.

CHAPTER EIGHT

THE MYTH OF "THE ONE"

September 2024

I stared at my phone screen for a full thirty seconds.

"Can you cover the mortgage this month? I can get you back by the 15th."

So, that text wasn't TO me. It was FROM me.

Which is . . . not ideal.

I'd been lying there for forty-three minutes, mentally rehearsing how to ask my own spouse to float me money for our bills. Not because of shame, in case you were wondering. (Well, maybe a little shame!) But mostly because of my pride at having supported myself for 41 years without having to ask someone for help.

I absolutely fucking hated it.

The root of my worries was for other reasons, and it was picking on me, frankly: the shape of my so-called portfolio career.

Other more tenured portfolio careerists that I followed online had much crisper narratives and portfolios:

"Full-time Fractional Something-or-Other" with a tidy client roster.

Or . . .

"Freelancer, Speaker, Coach, and Author of *5 Ways to Boss Up Your Life!*"

My portfolio was becoming a true patchwork. And now I was seriously considering adding a 9-5 job back into the mix to add an anchor income. (Going fractional just didn't appeal to me at the time.)

But because of that inkling to add back in a 9-5, it felt like I was doing this whole portfolio thing "wrong."

But then I caught myself mid thought: *"Wrong according to whom exactly? A portfolio career doesn't have a template, Brie. Take your own advice, why are you trying to force a model onto this!"*

This is my life, for crying out loud. Who gets to decide what I can and can't do but ME?

Although . . . maybe I should update my LinkedIn headline one more time.

———

I started job hunting in earnest that Fall, and I made a decision that went against every piece of career advice I'd recently received: I was going to tell the complete truth about what I'd been doing. That I had a side "hustle" that was non-negotiable for me to shut down.

My friend Sarah thought I'd lost my mind. "You can't tell employers you're running a business," she said to me over coffee. "You will never get a job, and you need one."

But I couldn't help myself. I needed this creative enterprise as much as I needed cash and insurance. Besides, I had a different perspective on the role a corporate job played in my life since I lost my job in 2023. I was a company-(wo)man no more. Yes, I'd do excellent work for fair pay, but I wasn't handing over my whole identity. Not this time.

Then when recruiters started to call and then ask about the ten-month gap in full-time employment, I would tell them exactly what I'd been doing. I celebrated the multi-faceted business I was building, as well as the skills and experiences it had afforded me.

After months of half-heartedly applying to jobs a few hours a week, I got hired by someone who very openly saw what I was doing on Linkedin and didn't seem to give a lick. Seriously, I DMed them via LinkedIn (from my very active and popping business-centered profile) and they didn't bat an eyelash at me as everyone had told me they would.

Three weeks later, I added a 9-5 job to my portfolio mix.

My first day was September 20th of 2024. I wore a blazer I'd bought for job interviews a year earlier. It still had the tags on it.

I felt myself nervously trying to slather my corporate veneer back on those first few days: straightening my posture and softening my opinions. Dialing into HR onboarding and team meetings, I felt like a bit of a cultural anthropologist. Everything looked familiar: the bright branding, the fancy software, the subtle knife of internal politics—but I was experiencing it all differently this time.

This job wasn't going to be my whole world. Just one piece of my portfolio. This was very strange.

I would catch myself observing my own reactions to things, as if from a distance.

How I related to this job felt so different. In my old corporate life, I brought every emotional need to work—validation, purpose, identity, social connection. And when the job couldn't hold all of that (because no job can!), I would end up feeling betrayed.

This time around though, I treated it for what it was: a mutually beneficial arrangement.

They needed strategic thinking and product marketing.

I needed income and health insurance.

A clean exchange.

And if they stopped needing me? My world wouldn't end.

I recognize that my style of portfolio career is strange to some.

Managing a full-time job plus my own multi-income stream business may sound impossible, I know. But don't forget, I had 10 months of building my business under my belt before I went back to a 9-to-5. And I don't have kids. That time out of corporate gave me the space to sit with my shit AND find product-market fit for my coaching practice, build an audience, get my content engine set up for social media, and plenty of practice running a podcast.

By the time I began this full-time job, I had business development, podcast production, and my frameworks down that running my business 10-15 hours a week felt as automatic and ingrained as brushing my teeth.

That's not to say it wasn't a hard transition. It for sure took some time getting used to. But it was doable.

My schedule became (and still is) a masterclass in time Tetris:

6 a.m.: Coffee and writing. This is non-negotiable. Before my brain gets colonized by other people's priorities, I reserve this hour for myself.

7:00 a.m.: Client calls 3-4x a week. Turns out I love early morning advisory meetings even as a non-morning person. I find it such a brilliant way to start the day before the chaos of corporate.

8:30 a.m. - 5:30 p.m.: Full on corporate citizen mode. Strategy meetings, project updates, etc.

6:00 p.m.: Decompression time with my family and dinner. A few nights a week, I'll do heavier administrative stuff for my business from my laptop, but I try to limit that to two nights a week, so that I don't burn out. Now, this means I have to ship a lot of imperfect things to honor my own need for rest time, but I am willing to ship B- work in the spirit of my selfcare.

Sunday afternoons: Batch editing podcast episodes, deep work on bigger business projects, sending clients notes, etc.

Was this sustainable? Depends on your definition. I prefer calling it integration versus balance.

Did it work for me, though? Surprisingly, *yes.*

Two months into working full time, though, I made a mistake thinking that I could handle more.

I decided to launch a digital course in the New Year, justifying the decision by thinking I already had the content for it. People kept asking for a more affordable way to work with me. How hard could it be to package everything into a DIY digital course?

Famous last words.

Turns out that building a course, layering in a full-time job, and maintaining a small business is like trying to renovate your kitchen while hosting dinner parties. Theoretically possible, practically insane.

I'd wake up at 5:45 a.m. for a coaching call, then immediately jump into a 9 a.m. strategy meeting, my brain still halfway in the last conversation. I'd schedule meetings about the course launch over lunch breaks, then realize I had not eaten anything yet that day.

December became a blur of late nights building course modules and marketing plans. Then I also had an unexpected move to Seattle thrown in there. Woof!

By the time January hit, I spent the month in what I now recognize was a depressive recovery state. I'd wake up exhausted, drag myself through the workday, come downstairs and stare blankly at my cats, unable to muster up motivation to play with them.

"What's wrong?" my best friend finally asked me.

"I don't know," I said. "I just . . . I can't do all of this anymore."

She smirked at me via FaceTime, "So stop doing some of it."

I smirked back.

It was at this point that I put course promotions on hold, scaled back my client load big time, and gave myself permission to just coast for a while—all in service of recharging my batteries. The relief was immediate. And course sales still rolled in despite the fact I wasn't trying as hard. A couple hundred bucks a month. Not bad for Energy Saver Mode!

Lesson learned, though: add one new thing at a time, even when you're excited and everything feels possible.

Point being, this career model isn't easy, even after you get going. You *will* overdo it from time to time, and you *will* have to adjust back to your own baseline when that happens. The key is having a decent sense of self-attunement and a community, which I mentioned earlier, to stop you from killing yourself just because you're jacked up on a tankful of intrinsic motivation.

———

When I layered in full-time work, something unexpected—and frankly terrifying—came up: I felt like I was cheating on my W-2 employer. It was as if taking on other projects while being contractually tied to a 9-to-5 was some form of professional infidelity.

Look, I'm not the first person to compare career relationships to romantic ones—and I won't be the last—but stay with me for a minute.

First of all, no one's partner should ever make them feel trapped.

And can we agree that the idea of "the one" is, at best, naive—and at worst, a toxic Hollywood trope? "The one" demands loyalty above all else. "The one" takes away your free will. "The one" leaves you stranded if your partner dies, leaves, or starts driving a Cybertruck.

Let the record show: I love my husband. I just refuse to believe we are required to be loyal to each other forever because of fate. Our agreement to be together is based on choosing each other—consciously and continuously—which feels far more romantic, don't you think?

Anyway, I was living in Portland at this part of my portfolio careering journey, which meant I had plenty of friends in nontraditional relationships, including lots of polyamorous folks. (You can't throw a donut in Portland without hitting someone's metamour!)

For those unfamiliar, polyamory is the practice of engaging in more than one romantic or intimate relationship at a time—with everyone's knowledge and consent. A metamour is your partner's partner—someone you may or may not be involved with directly.

For my polyamorous friends, there was never any notion of "the one." They found ways to get their needs met without putting all that pressure on a single relationship. Need a wild night out? That's Ivy. Want someone to cook dinner with? Leave Ivy out of the kitchen, and ask John to bring his spices!

And one day it hit me: portfolio careers are kind of like polyamory—*but for work.*

The difference between infidelity and polyamory is consent and clarity. Polyamory is an explicit agreement that says, "We will choose to get some of our needs met by other people sometimes."

When you've got a consulting practice, a part-time job, and a position on a board, you're not "cheating" on anyone if there is consent from your anchor employer—you're in what I like to call a *professional polycule.*

The word polycule comes from the queer and polyamorous community. In their book *It's Called Polyamory,* Tamara Pincus and Rebecca Hiles define polyamory as "a network of people in relationships with each other." In a professional context, a polycule means your growth isn't powered by one boss, mentor, or company—it's powered by a constellation of relationships that fuels your professional growth through collective wisdom, accountability, and shared abundance.

Now, for whatever reason, I happen to be wired for monogamy in my love life, but I couldn't help making this comparison when I think about how my career now looks today.

When I first got the courage to bring this up with my poly friends, the first thing they said was, "Brie, please don't name your book Professional Polyamory. For so many reasons, just . . . don't." But they also started building on the metaphor and pointed out how the methods for being a good poly partner could also be helpful in managing a portfolio career.

YOUR PROFESSIONAL
POLYCULE

ANCHOR EMPLOYER	Provide reliable income that supports you while you build other elements of your portfolio (e.g., a part-time role, fractional work, or W-2 job).
HYPE SQUAD	Cheer you on and affirm you formally (or informally) in your affinity communities of choice.
COLLABORATORS & CONNECTORS	Generous, well-networked people who open doors for you, introducing you to other partners and right fit opportunities that align with your goals.
SKILL BUILDERS	Your growth accelerators. People who help you develop your craft, offering constructive feedback, teach you new skills, or contribute their strengths to forward your body of work.
TRANSFORMATION AGENTS	Your accountability partners. Mentors, coaches, or peers who challenge you, push you, and help you follow through on your vision when things get hard.

Want FREE digital copies of the Polyworker frameworks?

Scan this QR code to download now.

The most obvious is that when poly people are "hinge partners" (i.e., in a relationship with multiple other people who are not dating each other), they quickly learn how to coordinate schedules. (That's how it works when managing multiple gigs and finding an anchor income stream.)

When poly people begin a new relationship, they have to manage the new relationship's impact on the relationships they're already in. (That's like bringing on a new income stream, creative project, or client.)

And, okay perhaps I run the risk of generalizing here, but when poly people are designing what they want their relationships to look like, they tend to work from more of a blank slate than monogamous people do. They pick and choose what belongs in a given relationship. They operate with fewer assumptions. They name their needs and boundaries with a kind of clarity that frequently takes me aback as a monog'. (Trust me, it'll catch on.)

The other parallel I see is that this style of romantic relationship is not for everyone, just as this style of work is not for everyone. You have to accept that, if you go down this path, not everyone is going to understand it because it's less mainstream.

Regardless, these are good skills to have!

Take a look at how this plays out on a few different levels:

Negotiation & Boundaries: Whether you're balancing clients or partners, you're actively consenting to give your time and energy to your relationships in a direct and honest way, which cultivates trust.

Agency & Choice: In both cases, you choose how to design your work around *your* values, interests, and capacity. The mix is intentional, not accidental. It requires deliberate negotiation. *You* are the author of your life.

Nonconformity & Originality: You might be misunderstood. People may see you as unstable or unfocused because you haven't defaulted to the normative options of monogamous hetero marriage or a 9-to-5 career path. Whether you're poly or a portfolio careerist, you're defying cultural expectations, and practitioners often face skepticism or judgment. On the other hand—you *will* find your people who do get it, and they will appreciate your commitment to being authentic, balanced, and intentional. Whose approval do you prefer—the people who like a balanced version of you or the people who prefer your mask?

Ethical Non-Monogamy: Not every employer will be okay with you having a portfolio career. So you need to proactively communicate this upfront to the companies prospecting you out of respect for both their time and yours.

Resilience & Diversification: Breakups always come with disappointment and grief, but when your system of support and meaning-making is distributed—you have a much better chance of being emotionally resilient as it is happening.

Depth vs. Breadth: Multiplicity doesn't mean shallowness, as some people might think. You're not giving fractions of your attention to any given relationship; you're identifying how to show up fully for each one of them based on their function. Some relationships—or in this case, roles—are deep, others want to be treated more lightly.

Self-identification as a Practice: In polyamory and in portfolio careerism, you craft a self that evolves over time, defined by being your own center of gravity and expressing yourself across diverse intimacies. Both are iterative practices of self-definition and growth over time. Again: you're ultimately choosing *yourself* as you hold space for your relationships to begin, end, and evolve over time.

Eventually, I found my rhythm again with these various parts of my portfolio career. And something magical started happening as a result: Each part of my portfolio made the other parts creatively sing! The insights from coaching clients informed my strategy work at the day job. The frameworks I developed for corporate projects became content for my newsletter. The challenges I wrote about in early essays became the genesis for this book.

It was like compound interest but for creativity.

This got me thinking: What would happen if I didn't have to hold out for "the one" professionally speaking anymore? What if "the one" who I was fated to choose . . . was me?

What would happen if I didn't have to hold out for "the one" professionally speaking anymore? What if "the one" who I was fated to choose . . . was me?

CHAPTER NINE

MAKING FRIENDS WITH THE PERFECTION GREMLIN

November 2024

I had just spent the entire day convincing myself that tomorrow—yes, TOMORROW!—I'd finally announce and launch my course on LinkedIn.

That I'd wake up with a jawline sharp enough to slice paper and have unshakable self-belief.

But tomorrow was here and instead I'm hunched over my laptop self-soothing with a bag of Swedish Fish obsessing over an announcement email. The unmistakable hum of the perfection gremlin lodged in my ear whispers to me, "*No, nooo, not ready, not ready. It is not good enough yet! Nooo . . .*"

I wash my hands before I retreat to ChatGPT for some sort of divine clarity for the 900th time. "What is the go-to market check-list for a digital course?"

My course launch had so many unknowns. And I had seen so much shit being peddled online—that overlapped with what I was offering in this course—for dirt cheap. Meanwhile, I'm trapped in my own self-perpetuated groundhog day loop of endless project research waiting for . . . what, exactly?

The universe to send me a divine signal that I was ready?

"Fuck. Fuck. Fuckfuckfuck," I mutter.

Then I did the only thing left to do: inhaled deeply, closed my eyes, and hit publish.

No trumpet blare, I am sad to report. No divine confirmation from the universe. Just me, alone in the glow of my laptop, relishing in birthing something that simultaneously excited and scared the crap out of me.

———

I used to think readiness would appear suddenly like a rom-com montage: decisive, glamorous, inevitable. I'd just wake up one day with perfect hair and the unwavering conviction of a TEDx speaker.

Readiness is the world's most sophisticated con artist. It dresses up like Responsibility but functions like that jealous Regina George-type friend who always tells you not to wear the crop top because "it's just not you" when it really *fucking* is you, you know?

There was zero shortage of people who were way less prepared than me, absolutely crushing it online. Were they any more "ready" than me? No. Absolutely not. But, they were *moving*. Forward. Sideways. Whatever way they went, they were in motion! Unlike me, who took up permanent residence in these moments inside my own head.

Eventually, I had to just . . . *decide* not to wait for clarity anymore. It felt weirdly presumptuous, and I was absolutely terrified. Like, full-scale nervous poops terrified. But fear didn't stop me.

Imposter syndrome is the bouncer at the door of growth. If you're not feeling a little like a fraud when you are trying something new, are you even *trying* something new?

In these moments of taking a leap of faith, your brain—bless its paranoid little self—starts scanning the universe, searching for a signal, a destination—*success*. So it fixates on people already at the finish line. This mental cruelty is biologically wired into us somehow: to fixate on people already at the finish line.

Look, feeling behind doesn't mean you *are* behind. It just means you care. A lot. This imposter feeling, the presence of that damn perfection gremlin—it isn't proof that you're unprepared. It's evidence you're pushing and growing the edges of your potential.

———

To be honest, I debated cutting this chapter from the book, but I kept it in because your inner critic is an *unchosen* colleague in these moments of self-transformation, lurking in the corners of that liminal space between who you are right now and who you're trying to become.

Designing your own CRM is a fucking breeze compared to the torture of that voice in your head whispering, *"Fraud!"* when your first Zapier automation fails. Sure, you can learn

Canva in an afternoon, but try recovering from discovering those typos *after* you've printed 200 copies of your workbook. And posting on LinkedIn? Easy. Coming to terms with zero likes and still believing you deserve to take up space online? That's the actual work.

This is why we idealize business gurus. They've achieved that nirvana state we're all chasing, and they seem so damn confident.

And yet . . . the only way through it is through it. You know?

There is no shortcut. You can't consume your way into being who you want to be. You can't get coached into certainty. You just have to move, inch by painful inch. Ship things before you feel ready. Say things out loud before the words are "perfect."

Confidence isn't a prerequisite of this process—it's a consequence. Those people you're comparing yourself to? Their brand isn't as polished as you think. (Trust me.) They just kept showing up, fully and messily, every single day, to this process of starting over. And they've made peace with being seen before they—and their ideas—are fully cooked.

That might be the hardest part of the beginning of this journey: allowing yourself to be witnessed mid-transformation, like an awkward teenager with a face full of pimples. There's such vulnerability in claiming an identity you're growing into. It'd be way easier to wait until you have proof, testimonials, fancy press, wouldn't it? A long trail of receipts to show the world (and yourself): *"See?! I AM legit."*

But what if the belief doesn't come before the receipts? Then what?

Imposter syndrome is the bouncer at the door of growth. If you're not feeling a little like a fraud when you are trying something new, are you even trying something new?

The version of me you met in Chapter 4–the one having a panic attack on my bathroom floor–feels like a past life.

But I'd be lying if I said she's gone entirely. I recognize her when she shows up, and boy, does she *show up*–conveniently, every time I take a bold step toward some new form of creativity in my portfolio. The difference now is that I've made friends with her. Or at least, we've reached a détente.

So don't get it twisted: I haven't achieved some permanent state of professional enlightenment. I still have bad days, difficult clients, moments of existential career doubt. But now I have things I'd never had before: options and self-belief.

If coaching gets overwhelming, I can dial it back for a month or two and focus more on writing. If the day job starts feeling soul-crushing, I have other projects and income streams to fall back on for a spiritual boost. If I want to experiment with something new, I have the financial means to try it out without risking my ability to pay my bills.

Now I have proof that things get hard before they get easy. That my intuition is never wrong. And those big girl pants? They get more comfortable putting back on when I need to.

Two years into this journey, I have dreams that feel possible instead of just wishful. A second book. Maybe a third! Community events that bring my people together. Corporate speaking engagements. Big, scary public conversations that change how we think about work and life integration.

The best part in all of this is that it feels so open ended which is freeing as fuck. Next year might look completely different from this year. Maybe I'll find a different job that fits better with my portfolio. Maybe I'll phase out the day job entirely. Or maybe I'll hold steady with what I'm doing for another year.

The point is, I get to *choose* where this goes.

For the first time in my professional life, I'm not trapped by my decisions. I'm empowered by them.

━━━━━━━━

We lose so much time waiting for our readiness.

We don't talk enough about the cost of this waiting. We frame it as noble or careful, but every time you defer your new beginning, you chip away at your trust in yourself. You reinforce this idea that your instincts can't be trusted or counted on.

I wrote this chapter as much for you as for the version of myself that needed these same words 18 months ago. The middle-aged millennial in a quiet crisis who over researched and analyzed EVERYTHING. Who was, frankly, convinced the internet would collectively point and laugh if she started building a business before she had everything all figured out.

Fast forward to today, here is what I know is true:

You don't need to know how it all ends.

You just need to stop waiting for proof before you believe in yourself and *start* something.

Please, release the "fake it till you make it" mantra. You're not faking anything, honey. You're taking the life you have lived so far and are pointing it in a new direction. That's not pretending, that's evolution.

Maybe it's time to say, not with bravado, but with embodied decisiveness: *"Fuggit. I'm just gonna do this!"* And act like you mean it.

If there is an idea that won't leave you alone—for a business, a book, a creative project—that's not a coincidence. That's a calling that you will honor eventually.

So why not honor it *right now*?

Don't worry about having credentials or a fully baked plan. You just need to ask yourself one question every day: What's one small thing I can do today to make this idea more real?

Then ask yourself that again the next day.

And the next day.

And the next.

That's how a body of work is born and businesses are built.

Start today.

You've been ready this whole fucking time.

You don't need to know how it all ends. You just need to stop waiting for proof before you believe in yourself and start something.

ARCHITECTS OF THE AFTERWARD

October 2025

If you made it this far in the book–thank you. Genuinely. I can be a bit . . . much. (Pithy, poetic, occasionally allergic to brevity!). You deserve a goddamn medal.

Jokes aside, I wrote this book to make sense of a moment in the sophomore chapter of my portfolio career that demanded interrogation. In the Spring of 2024, portfolio careers were seemingly everywhere–neatly packaged as the cure to modern work. Everyone had become an expert overnight, complete with courses, frameworks, and "proven systems." And there I was, thinking, "Oh God. Am I becoming one of those people?"

I wrote this book to wrestle with that question. I guess I could have sparred with ChatGPT about it all, but instead I spent a good three months working with an incredible writing coach, actually sitting down and putting pen to paper, trying to figure out what this whole present day portfolio career movement was really about. And if I was potentially selling fucking snake oil!

The strange thing about writing a book like this is that you spend months alone with your thoughts, convinced you're the only one asking these sort of questions. Then your creation goes out into the world, and your readers react to it—and you realize: this wasn't just my story, it was *our* story. Somehow, in trying to make sense of my own messy middle, I'd created something that might help other people make sense of theirs too in this unique moment in human history.

I'm still figuring this all out, to be honest. Some days I feel like a true portfolio careerist. Other days I feel like I'm just holding things together with duct tape and a sliver of hope like a polyworker. But here's what I know now that I didn't know when I started writing this thing: This book matters. Not because portfolio careers are the answer to everything—they're not. But because choosing to live deliberately, to work consciously, and to reclaim the parts of ourselves we thought we had to trade away—that's worth talking about, writing about, and coaching about. Even when it's messy. Especially when it's messy.

So whether you are in Act, I, II, III, or IV of your own professional reinvention, wondering if you are going to be okay—this is me telling you that you are doing great and that it's okay to build something that doesn't look like anyone else's blueprint.

You only get one life. ONE. Don't spend it chasing someone else's definition of success.

Your move, superstar. Choose wisely.

ENJOYING THIS BOOK SO FAR?

SUPPORT AN INDIE AUTHOR!

I am so grateful for my committed and loyal readers! Your reviews are some of the best thank-yous I can receive.

Reviews are the most powerful tool I have as an author when it comes to bringing my books to the attention of other readers.

If you enjoyed this book, I would be very grateful if you could spend just five minutes leaving a review on Amazon or Goodreads (it can be as short as you like) and/or share your experience with the book with the internet.

INTEGRATING

So... how exactly do you begin building a portfolio career?

Don't kill the messenger. Two words: *It depends.*

Not the answer you wanted, I know. But it's the truth. Your version of a successful portfolio career won't look like mine. In fact, your goal shouldn't be to follow my path towards a portfolio career–it's to figure out what works for your specific combination of skills, circumstances, and dreams.

That's why the last "act" of this book is a reflection workbook to help you integrate what you've read and start developing a portfolio career for *your* specific context.

I've arranged it as a collection of exercises, which represent some of the most common story beats that come up for nearly every polyworker turned portfolio careerist I've encountered.

Let's get weird.

Prefer a digital copy of this workbook?

Scan this QR code to download it instantly.

EXERCISE #1

LOOK AT YOUR INTERNAL STORIES

How do you currently define success?

What gets labeled as "high achievement" in your field? What milestones or accomplishments tend to earn recognition? What impresses the people around you? Who in your industry seems to have figured it out?

What (if anything) is standing in your way of success?

What is currently making these conventional goals harder to reach? What have you thought you needed to change about yourself? What do you imagine others might perceive as your limitations?

____

____

____

____

____

____

____

____

____

Stop here. Don't look at the next page until you've reflected about both question-clusters above.

". . . if our bookshelves are where we telegraph a version of who we want to be, then our YouTube search histories, culled from late hours punching away at whiskey-soaked keyboards, are what we really are, the self that is led by desire rather than decorum."

–Jonathan Goldstein, "Why Is Mason Reese Crying?" Heavyweight, October 8, 2020.

Your first opportunity, dear polyworker, invites you to trace the origins of your answers from the previous page.

Start with what's most visible: Can you recall specific sources–people, institutions, experiences–that shaped your definition of "success" or suggested particular paths you "should" follow?

Think of this like creating a map of influences or assembling a bibliography.

Next, go a little deeper: who or what reinforces your ideas about success? Look at the media you've collected. The TV shows you watch impulsively, and, yes, your YouTube search history (or TikTok algorithm, or Substack feed).

(Remember how I severely over-analyzed *Mad Men* in chapter 2? What piece of media could serve as your way-too-neat vision of "success?")

____

____

____

____

____

If you're feeling really saucy (and you're sufficiently therapized), identify where some of your family's stories about success come from.

____

____

____

____

____

Hey, look at that: "success" is just a story that you tell yourself, and it comes from somewhere specific.

But it's not an objective truth. There are other stories you can tell yourself now!

TWIDDLE THE KNOBS OF YOUR GIVE-A-FUCK BUDGET

Remember, in Chapter 5, how I told you about the time I documented what I had been doing with my time? I sat cross-legged on the living room floor and documented everything?

Don't do that.

Not yet.

Read all of these exercises first. (I'm saving the best for last: I'll give you the template for the portfolio career canvas at the end!)

First, I want you to project how much time you want to spend doing your most frequent activities in a typical week. It'll sound like:

- I want to spend 50 hours sleeping each week.

- I want to spend 10 hours investing in building my business each week.

- I want to spend 4 hours responding to messages each week.

- I want to spend 15 hours attending meetings each week.

These should be a combination of things that you are absolutely obligated to do, things that you prioritize highly, and things that are necessary to maintain your life.

If it's helpful to simplify the "categories" of how you spend time, you can combine unique tasks into broad buckets.

- Singing lullabies + bathtime + managing tantrums = Attuning to my toddler

- Smoking weed + staring into space + stress-eating white cheddar popcorn = Worrying

- Rewriting Miranda's explosively offensive emails + jumping in to manage Howard's Zoom meetings + manning the front desk because Claudine has cramps = Work snafus

You're a smartie, so you probably see where this is going.

Next you're going to actually measure how much time you spend doing these things in a typical week.

"But my life is so chaotic. There's no such thing as a typical week!" I hear you saying through the metaphysical author-reader portal.

Fine. Do it four times and average them out. The point isn't to be accurate; it's to get a dose of reality.

It's going to look like this:

- I actually spend 45 hours sleeping each week, but I want to spend 50 hours.

- I actually spend 5 hours investing in building my business each week, but I want to spend 10 hours.

- I actually spend 7 hours responding to messages each week, but I want to spend 4 hours.

- I actually spend 24 hours attending meetings each week, but I want to spend 15 hours.

Next step: a wee bit of math and a big bit of goal-setting.

There will probably be a difference between your preferred schedule and your actual schedule. You won't be able to snap your fingers and change all of your habits. At least I really don't think so.

Instead I want you to make small shifts that build upon your existing habits and tools.

Sustained commitment at a pace you can manage will build durable habits much better than an attempt at wholesale reinvention, which usually falls apart pretty quickly.

Choose to change one thing (per category) each week.

It's going to look like this:

- I actually spend 45 hours sleeping each week, but I want to spend 50 hours, so I will figure out how to change the settings on my phone, so it becomes useless at 9pm.

- I actually spend 5 hours investing in building my business each week, but I want to spend 10 hours, so I will take Brandon up on his accountability group.

- I actually spend 7 hours responding to messages each week, but I want to spend 4 hours, so I will ask the most-high-maintenance person in my inbox to schedule a call instead of emailing me 10 times in one day.

- I actually spend 24 hours attending meetings each week, but I want to spend 15 hours, so I will withdraw from that time-consuming committee.

If this feels helpful, you can keep twiddling the knobs of your give-a-fuck budget using a simplified no-math version.

- I want to spend less time trolling job listings so I will reinvest that time sending targeted emails.

- I want to spend more time doing deep work so I will rejigger my Calendly availability to reserve 2-4pm each day.

A funny thing happens when you rehearse these sentences: you start saying them out loud and, thus, reminding other people what matters to you and why setting boundaries will help you do that.

It's kind of a flex.

(But try not to be an asshole about it. The most high-maintenance person in your inbox probably doesn't need to know that they earned that superlative.)

Alternate version: Instead of listing your most-frequent activities, break down how your time is spent across the six forms of labors described in the Portfolio Career Canvas in Chapter 6. As a reminder, they are:

- Wage Work

- Caregiving

- Acts of Service

- Upskilling

- Experiments

- Self-Care

Identify what your goals are for the next "season" of your life. (I happen to like setting goals in 3-month intervals, because I work in seasons and this amount of time is generally how long it takes for an experiment to provide a useful signal.)

Perhaps the next few months are a good time to invest more of your time experimenting and setting firmer boundaries around your tendency to perform self-care (and not actually recharge). Or maybe you need to double down on building up some revenue through wage work and forego some of the socializing for a week or two.

TEMPLATE

I actually spend _____ hours doing _____ each week, but I want to spend _____ hours, so I will _____.

NO-MATH VERSION:

I want to spend (more/less) time doing _____, so I will _____.

PUT ON YOUR RED LIPSTICK

This one starts with a story.

One time, I was out dancing with friends, and I saw this distractingly attractive woman tearing up the dance floor. She was impossible to miss. She was a vision in red: gorgeous dress, a cool-ass hipster haircut, super cute earrings.

And fire engine red lipstick.

Man after man made his way over to her to try his chances with her.

Each time, she'd smile politely and then turn away. Sometimes a guy would wait around nearby, but eventually he'd get the hint.

One of these Romeos stuck around for a few minutes and kept inching closer to her. Eventually she said something directly into his ear that prompted the guy to back off and go rejoin his friend, who was sitting near me at the bar.

"I asked her if she wanted to dance," Romeo said. "She said she's dancing on her own."

Dear reader, that woman was Robyn, and that is how the song *Dancing On My Own* came into being.

(Just kidding, it wasn't Robyn.)

But I think about that woman in the red lipstick all the time.

What would it mean to do something completely for your creative self for an evening?

I want you to do three things:

1. Schedule time that you are designating as unstructured. Clear away all obligations. You are not fitting this in on the same night that you are keeping an eye on laundry and, oh yeah, need to throw something together for dinner. You might like to choose a night when you know you'll have lots of options of things you like to do, but I recommend against committing yourself to anything in particular.

2. Make yourself unavailable. This is a different thing than not having any obligations. The woman in the red dress didn't just go on the dance floor without an intention to dance with someone, she also had the intention to not dance with anyone.

3.   Put on something special. Maybe red lipstick. Maybe an old bracelet. Maybe a ring from a vending machine. It doesn't have to be sexy or glam; it just has to be something you wouldn't normally wear. Put it on to indicate to yourself that this is your red lipstick time.

Try to authentically engage your creative passions. Were you a musician in a previous part of your life? Go check out a live band. Has it been a while since you've been to a museum? I bet there's a free night at the one nearest you. When was the last time you went for a walk in nature? It turns out that trees and birds still exist (as of this publication, anyway)!

This is a hard, hard thing to do for codependent people who struggle to answer mean questions like, "What do you want for dinner?" or "What are you in the mood to do tonight?"

If you need additional guidance, I recommend reading Julia Cameron's *The Artist's Way* and learning about the Artist's Date ritual, which she discusses in the early sections of the book.

EXERCISE #4

ASSEMBLE THE POLYCULE

Part 1

Time for some fan fiction.

Imagine that you can choose exactly six characters—from across the wide spectrum of workplace comedies—to be the handful of people you work with most frequently.

That's right. We're casting your hype-squad, your collaborators, and your connectors, etc.—the people who are going to support you on your first experiment in your portfolio. (Or, for you over-achieving corporate types, your personal board of directors!)

Have fun with this. Follow your sense of joy. But also try to pick people who you think you would genuinely and successfully work well with and that would support you specifically for the goals you have for your portfolio for the next six to nine months.

Keep it to six people and remember that a good ensemble cast has a balance of types.

If you're not much of a TV/movie person . . . fine. Choose from your other preferred pool of "characters." Maybe it's any person you've ever known, living or dead and at any age. Which means you could team up your late great-uncle Stosh at age 26 with your college roommate at age 35.

Now that you've put together this fantasy roster, identify the two to three main, broad qualities that make each character a good colleague. Not what makes them funny. Not what makes them a great character. Not what makes them good at their job. Why would they *actually* be a solid person to work with day-in and day-out for years?

Maybe you wrote down Leslie Knope from *Parks and Recreation*, because Amy Poehler is brilliant at playing a relentless worker and friend. But perhaps the reason you'd want her in your professional polycule is because of the way she can provide a clear sense of direction for an initiative.

Maybe you wrote down Jim Halpert from *The Office*, because Jon Krasinski is just so good to look at—at any age— and he's also effortlessly funny. But then what makes him an ideal colleague in your eyes might be that he's an ideal person to witness workplace challenges with, because he sees exactly what you're seeing.

Once you've done this, take away the characters' names and just look at this initial support network.

Do you need someone who provides a sense of direction? Do you need someone who is witnessing your experience with you? Do you have someone that knows a lot more about AI automations than you currently do?

That kinda thing.

Score the collective qualities of your current colleagues against this rubric. You can score out of 5 or score out of 100 or give it a letter grade. It doesn't matter. Whatever's meaningful to you.

Part 2

One of the reasons why networking can feel so cringe is because it's often so aimless.

If I never go to another networking event with a goddamn fucking stupid Bingo card, it'll be too soon.

You're going into this with intentionality.

Pick one of the characters or character qualities with a low score on the rubric. Make an action plan for engaging in a community that already exists and that likely contains a few people with that particular energy.

If it were Pokémon, you'd know to look for a water type in the ocean or search for a bug type in the woods. (I don't know, you might have to ask my godchild about that one.)

In the polyworker school of networking, you may have to be a bit more creative.

Looking for an inspiring figure in an industry or movement you care about? Go to some lectures. You might not meet the keynote speaker, but you might sit next to an interesting person who's doing cool stuff you hadn't heard of.

Looking for commiseration? Join a Slack community that's organized by people in your line of work. You might not (definitely won't) keep up with all of the messages, but you might stumble on a thinkpiece-writer who's the voice of a generation.

Try not to be too rigid about what you're looking for and how these relationships take shape. It's never useful to try to box people into a slot that you've assigned for them. Just let this community organically turn into something in time. Make a point once you've defined your support system to engage with these people formally or informally, so you have what you need to get going.

INTERCEPT THE BOUNCER

In Chapter 9, I refer to imposter syndrome as the "bouncer at the door of growth." (It's classy to quote yourself, isn't it?)

We're gonna do some roleplay now.

I hope you have a friend with a theatre degree, because I'm going to suggest you recruit somebody who isn't afraid to do some improv with you (and who is also sensitive and attuned enough to hold space for difficult emotions that may come up in this exercise).

I want you to see what happens when you try each of the following two scenarios:

1. **You play the bouncer. Your scene partner plays you.**

You get to say, out loud to your scene partner, all of the things that this bouncer (your sense of imposter syndrome) says to you in your mind. Go through the whole laundry list. Try to say them all.

Your scene partner's job is to listen and say, "Whatever?" every now and then.

Notice that when you embody the bouncer, you say things that you would never even think to say to a person you respect. After a while, it starts to feel ridiculous.

That's the point.

You might find yourself saying, "You can't join that club because you don't post enough on LinkedIn!"

And when your scene partner looks back at you with a look like WTF . . . How can you not realize how ridiculous that bouncer is in the end?

2. You play you. Your scene partner plays the bouncer.

Your scene partner's job is to try to sound objective as they tell you why you're not allowed in. They're spouting off criteria that are listed plainly on their clipboard.

Your job is to argue your way in. Be as brash and brave as you can.

"I can't let you through, because it says here you need a master's degree to be a legitimate founder," the bouncer might say.

And you can say, "Oh, fuck off. Plenty of CEOs don't have masters degrees, and that doesn't preclude them from being complete schmucks."

In both games, the joke is on the bouncer.

If you don't feel like role playing live, try writing letters in-character—or recording voice memos.

GOOD-ENOUGH FOR VERSION ONE

This last exercise is a good one for any time you're preparing to start something: a side hustle, a business, a brand, or a new project in your portfolio.

It starts with a simple question: Define what version one of that business, brand, or project would look like for you.

V1: Version one, the smallest possible version of the thing that would still be whole. The least common denominator. The minimum viable product. The point at which it goes from nothing to something. From an idea to a thing.

Here's what your V1 might look like:

- A simple website where a potential client can book a free call with you.

- A coaching "product" (could be a simple PDF) that you begin beta-testing within your network.

- An Etsy shop where someone could, presumably, buy your throwaway sketches.

- A weekly schedule in which you designate time for market research and networking calls to figure out WTF you want to do next with your career.

I have a few recommendations of how to think about the "minimum viable" part:

- It shouldn't require an investment that feels like a sacrifice. It shouldn't interfere with other parts of your life in a consequential way.

- It's low-stakes. There's no inherent riskiness.

- It's probably not going to be broadly visible.

- It won't require other people to invest tons of their own resources. For example, you might be providing value at no or low cost.

- If it doesn't work out, you won't be devastated.

Once you figure out what that is, go ahead and schedule a "check-in" conversation with yourself a week or two from now. This gives you enough time to make V1 happen.

During that "check-in" conversation, notice what you learned from the experience of making V1.

Ask yourself: what do we do next, boss?

ARE YOU PORTFOLIO CAREER CURIOUS?

Ready to go even deeper in building your portfolio career? Scan this QR Code to get in touch with Brie.

ABOUT THE AUTHOR

Brianne Abramowicz spent the first half of her career in leadership positions at Bank of America, Amazon, Target, and a variety of venture-backed startups, commercializing and repositioning over 25 businesses. Her products have been featured in WIRED, DIELINE, The New York Times, The Spoon, Food Dive, and New Rules Media.

Somewhere along the way, she realized most people–including herself–were building careers the same way bad products get built: without conviction and by external committee. Then in 2023, she took on the scariest reinvention of them all: her own, founding *Build with Brie Creative*, a boutique product marketing studio that helps multi-hyphenate founders, creatives, and professionals in transition position their businesses and portfolio careers.

Her first book, *Polyworker*, is an honest reflection of her experience accidentally building a portfolio career. It's become a go-to for professionals who are ready to reinvent their careers on their terms.

These days you can catch her helping wildly talented humans find a little more joy and ease in their work, chasing epic views—and even better snacks—somewhere in the Olympics with her husband. They live in Seattle with their two tuxedo cats, Momo and Stout.

A NOTE ON INTELLECTUAL LINEAGE

While this book draws on Charles Handy's articulation of the portfolio career model, I want to note that my thinking is also deeply shaped by the work of bell hooks, whose contributions deserve explicit acknowledgment here.

In her work, bell consistently emphasized that systems of domination—racism, sexism, classism, and patriarchy—are inseparable. One cannot be dismantled without confronting the others. Long before "intersectionality" entered mainstream discourse, she challenged forms of feminism that centered white, middle-class women while ignoring class struggle, racial hierarchy, and economic exploitation. Her work insisted on a feminism that was structural, relational, and anti-capitalist.

So although she did not write about portfolio careers directly, her insistence on wholeness, dignity, and liberation beyond narrow economic participation profoundly informs the moral and philosophical foundations of this book. Because where Handy offered a structural reimagining of work, hooks offered the necessary critique of power—one that reminds us that new working models must not simply rearrange freedom for the already-privileged, but also expand it for those historically excluded.